NEW DIRECTIONS FOR EVALUATION
A PUBLICATION OF THE AMERICAN EVALUATION ASSOCIATION

Gary T. Henry, *Georgia State University*
COEDITOR-IN-CHIEF

Jennifer C. Greene, *University of Illinois*
COEDITOR-IN-CHIEF

Information Technologies in Evaluation: Social, Moral, Epistemological, and Practical Implications

Geri Gay
Cornell University

Tammy L. Bennington
Cornell University

EDITORS

Number 84, Winter 1999

JOSSEY-BASS PUBLISHERS
San Francisco

H
62
A1
V84
1999

INFORMATION TECHNOLOGIES IN EVALUATION: SOCIAL, MORAL, EPISTEMO-
LOGICAL, AND PRACTICAL IMPLICATIONS
Geri Gay, Tammy L. Bennington (eds.)
New Directions for Evaluation, no. 84
Jennifer C. Greene, Gary T. Henry, Coeditors-in-Chief
Copyright ©1999 Jossey-Bass Inc., Publishers, 350 Sansome Street, San
Francisco, CA 94104.

Microfilm copies of issues and articles are available in 16mm and 35mm,
as well as microfiche in 105mm, through University Microfilms Inc., 300
North Zeeb Road, Ann Arbor, Michigan 48106-1346.

New Directions for Evaluation is indexed in Contents Pages in Education,
Higher Education Abstracts, and Sociological Abstracts.

ISSN 1097-6736   ISBN 0-7879-4904-3

NEW DIRECTIONS FOR EVALUATION is part of The Jossey-Bass Education
Series and is published quarterly by Jossey-Bass Inc., Publishers, 350 Sansome Street, San Francisco, California 94104-1342.

SUBSCRIPTIONS cost $65.00 for individuals and $118.00 for institutions,
agencies, and libraries. Prices subject to change.

EDITORIAL CORRESPONDENCE should be addressed to the Editors-in-Chief,
Jennifer C. Greene, Department of Educational Psychology, University of
Illinois, 260E Education Building, 1310 South Sixth Street, Champaign,
IL 61820, or Gary T. Henry, School of Policy Studies, Georgia State Uni-
versity, P.O. Box 4039, Atlanta, GA 30302-4039.

www.josseybass.com

Printed in the United States of America on acid-free recycled paper containing 100 percent recovered waste paper, of which at least 20 percent is
postconsumer waste.

Editorial Policy and Procedures

New Directions for Evaluation, a quarterly sourcebook, is an official publication of the American Evaluation Association. The journal publishes empirical, methodological, and theoretical works on all aspects of evaluation. A reflective approach to evaluation is an essential strand to be woven through every volume. The editors encourage volumes that have one of three foci: (1) craft volumes that present approaches, methods, or techniques that can be applied in evaluation practice, such as the use of templates, case studies, or survey research; (2) professional issue volumes that present issues of import for the field of evaluation, such as utilization of evaluation or locus of evaluation capacity; (3) societal issue volumes that draw out the implications of intellectual, social, or cultural developments for the field of evaluation, such as the women's movement, communitarianism, or multiculturalism. A wide range of substantive domains is appropriate for *New Directions for Evaluation;* however, the domains must be of interest to a large audience within the field of evaluation. We encourage a diversity of perspectives and experiences within each volume, as well as creative bridges between evaluation and other sectors of our collective lives.

The editors do not consider or publish unsolicited single manuscripts. Each issue of the journal is devoted to a single topic, with contributions solicited, organized, reviewed, and edited by a guest editor. Issues may take any of several forms, such as a series of related chapters, a debate, or a long article followed by brief critical commentaries. In all cases, the proposals must follow a specific format, which can be obtained from the editor-in-chief. These proposals are sent to members of the editorial board and to relevant substantive experts for peer review. The process may result in acceptance, a recommendation to revise and resubmit, or rejection. However, the editors are committed to working constructively with potential guest editors to help them develop acceptable proposals.

Jennifer C. Greene, Coeditor-in-Chief
Department of Educational Psychology
University of Illinois
260E Education Building
1310 South Sixth Street
Champaign, IL 61820
e-mail:jcgreene@uiuc.edu

Gary T. Henry, Coeditor-in-Chief
School of Policy Studies
Georgia State University
P.O. Box 4039
Atlanta, GA 30302-4039
e-mail: gthenry@gsu.edu

CONTENTS

EDITORS' NOTES

The current proliferation of information technologies and computer-mediated communication tools is transforming the organizational settings, programs, and professional networks with and within which evaluators work. Evaluators increasingly find themselves involved in evaluating new technologies, computer-delivered programs, human-computer interactions, and computer-mediated organizational practices and relations. Evaluation activities such as the collection, management, analysis, and representation of data are all increasingly mediated through electronic tools. This volume of *New Directions for Evaluation* attempts to raise awareness of the implications of technology for evaluation practice and to stimulate dialogue regarding the social, moral, epistemological, and practical dimensions of emerging technologies and computer-mediated evaluation methods.

In the first chapter, the editors introduce activity theory as a useful conceptual framework and vocabulary with which to understand the situated use of diverse technologies in the emerging, technologically textured landscape of evaluation. They draw attention to the potential benefits as well as potential shortcomings of various computer-mediated data collection technologies and how technologies and the social contexts in which they are employed reciprocally mediate and transform one another.

The contributions of Watt and of Rieger and Sturgill identify how various computer-based technologies enable inquirers to collect and analyze data in new and unique ways and through emerging electronic environments. Watt provides a comprehensive overview of the research potential of the Internet as an evaluation tool and setting. He details the advantages, disadvantages, and practical challenges of conducting e-mail questionnaires, Web-based surveys, and Web-based focus groups. Understanding Web-based tools and data collection methods is of increasing practical relevance as access to the Internet increases and as more and more services and information are provided on-line. Rieger and Sturgill explore the use of technology to evaluate technology, addressing various methods for recording user-computer interactions and for collecting feedback on electronic systems from users and designers as they engage with systems on-line.

The chapter by Bennington, Gay, and Jones explores how today's technologies facilitate the integration of observations, interview data, and video and audio records into multimedia databases and texts and how multimedia applications can foster mixed-method research designs, as well as collaborative and participatory inquiry. Mathison, Meyer, and Vargas provide a historical, methodological, and philosophical overview of the use of verbal protocols in the evaluation of computer hardware and software. To redress the problematic assumptions of information processing that inform verbal protocol methodology, they advocate its contextualization within a cultural-historical activity theory framework that highlights the social embeddedness of technologies.

In the final chapter Bennington considers the ethical implications of the aforementioned technologies, exploring how their use obligates evaluators to reconceptualize traditional ethical concerns such as anonymity, confidentiality, prevention of harm, and disposition of data. She again draws upon the activity theory model to understand the ethical dimensions of technology-use in terms of the social relations among evaluation participants.

This volume is intended to provide an introduction to various emerging technologies and tools, from off-the-shelf applications to sophisticated collaborative groupware, that can provide new insights into the complex interactions that constitute an increasingly technologically mediated evaluation inquiry. Computer technologies enable inquirers to collect, analyze, and present data in new and unique ways and allow the integration of observations, video and audio records, documents, and more. They thereby encourage new ways of knowing, but simultaneously pose new responsibilities and obligations for evaluators. A thread running through the issue, as expressed by the several authors who invoke activity theory, is the need to understand the use of technology in evaluation inquiry as it mediates and is mediated by the social contexts of that use.

GERI GAY is associate professor in the department of communications at Cornell University and director of the Human-Computer Interaction Group at Cornell.

TAMMY L. BENNINGTON is research associate in the Human-Computer Interaction Group at Cornell University and adjunct professor in the Program on Social and Organizational Learning at George Mason University.

1

Evaluation inquiry is increasingly mediated by the use of complex electronic technologies such as Web-based communication tools, multimedia applications, and electronic tracking devices. Activity theory provides a useful conceptual framework with which to understand the epistemological, practical, and moral implications of that mediation.

Reflective Evaluation in a "Technologically Textured" World: An Activity Theory Approach

Geri Gay, Tammy L. Bennington

The proliferation of computer and information technologies over the past decade has begun to transform the landscape of evaluation research practices. Data collection can now include Web-based surveys, computer-mediated synchronous and asynchronous communication applications, and reliance on organizational information systems and intranets. Evaluators have become proficient in the use of diverse computer technologies for quantitative data analysis, and increasingly for qualitative analysis (NUD*IST, QUALPRO, Folio Views, NVivo, etc.). Because of the pervasiveness of computer artifacts and computer-mediated communication in programs and evaluation activities, we might say, following Ihde (1990, p. 1), that our lives as evaluators are "technologically textured." Evaluation activities are embedded in complex technosystems that have significantly shaped how evaluations are designed and conducted. We use computer technologies and their multimedia functionalities for the collection of (multimedia) data, for their organization and analysis, and for our composition, presentation, and dissemination of findings. Various groupware applications, for example, LotusNotes or Trochim's (n.d.) concept-mapping package (<http://trochim.human.cornell.edu/research/epp1/epp1.htm>), can facilitate collaboration among evaluators and stakeholders, new ways of conducting evaluations, the integration of methods, as well as organizational learning through formative evaluation.

New technologies provide opportunities for developing innovative evaluation tools that can enable the collection of new kinds of information, for example, computer tracking applications that reveal users' keystroke-by-keystroke actions. New technologies also enable new forms of data management, analysis, and presentation via applications that integrate digital video, audio, text, and graphics. These tools can disclose behaviors and social phenomena that have remained hidden and unexamined (for example, how a person navigates a social service's website), because the technologies required to reveal them—or, depending on your ontological and epistemological views, to "construct" them—did not exist. Because new technologies enable new ways of knowing, evaluating, and representing and reporting knowledge, they pose methodological, social, and ethical challenges that require reflection and action on the part of evaluators. Drawing upon Cornell University's Human-Computer Interaction Group's extensive experience with evaluating technologies in use (Kilker and Gay, 1998; Mead and Gay, 1995), we attempt in this article to navigate a pragmatic yet critical position intermediate between the utopian and dystopian perspectives that tend to polarize discussions of technology and multimedia (see Nardi and O'Day, 1999). We lay out a theoretical framework that accommodates a complex understanding of the multiple, often contradictory, implications of new technologies for evaluation practice. We draw upon what we consider the potential opportunities provided by these technologies, but with caution, simultaneously reflecting upon what these technologies occlude, exclude, and conceal. Our objective is to provoke critical awareness that can inform the evaluator's selection and assessment of technologies and tools in particular use contexts.

Activity Theory and the Mediating Function of Technology

We have found activity theory a useful conceptual framework for understanding the role of technology both in program delivery and evaluation and for anticipating the social implications of technology use in different contexts. Activity theory is an integrative and holistic approach to human behavior and learning that derives from the work of Vygotsky, Leont'ev, Luria, and the Russian social psychological tradition. It is particularly useful for studying intentional actions that are directed toward the achievement of a goal, the accomplishment of a task, or the realization of a possibility. We will briefly describe activity theory as it has been taken up by researchers in the field of human-computer interaction (Nardi, 1996), and we focus on socially situated tool use and tool mediation. Mathison, Meyer, and Vargas later in this volume present activity theory from a slightly different social-psychological perspective, focusing on its explication of the relationship among cognition, speech, and social context as relevant to verbal protocol methodology.

In activity theory, the "activity" provides the fundamental unit of analysis, or "minimal meaningful context" (Kuutti, 1996). An activity is motivated by a desire to achieve a particular objective (see Figure 1.1). The boundaries of activities are inherently ambiguous and can be understood as practical, heuristic, or even rhetorical circumscriptions; activities can overlap or can merge as objectives are transformed or as relevant contexts change. For example, data collection as an activity often merges imperceptibly into data analysis in practice, but can be distinguished for analytical, didactic, or practical purposes. Or the evaluative inquiry project as a whole can be identified as an activity (Figure 1.2).

An *activity* entails individual or group agency (the *subject*) and the subject's use of tools to achieve desired or intended goals (the *object*). It is situated within a broader social context that entails particular community norms, values, division of labor, and social structures. The subject's relationship with and orientation toward an objective is mediated by tools/artifacts, the community participating in the activity, and the division of labor in that community (Bellamy, 1996, p. 125). In the above model, the bi-directional arrows are used to indicate multiple mutually mediating relationships, representing a complex integrated system. Fundamental premises of activity theory pertinent to our current purpose of understanding tool use in evaluation include (1) unity of consciousness and activity, (2) object-orientedness, and (3) the *mediating* role of tools (Kaptelinin, 1996, pp. 107–109).

Kaptelinin (1996, p. 107) notes that human consciousness "emerges and exists as a special component of human interactions with the environment." How we know or understand the world and how we engage with the world are mutually constitutive processes. The implications, in regards to evaluation, are that evaluators, through the pragmatic activities in which they engage, the questions they pose, and the conceptual, methodological, and technological tools they employ, develop particular ways of perceiving and understanding the world. It is therefore a useful exercise to critically

Figure 1.1. The Activity Theory Model

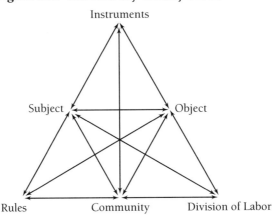

Adapted from Kuutti (1996), p. 28. Used by permission.

Figure 1.2. Evaluation as Activity

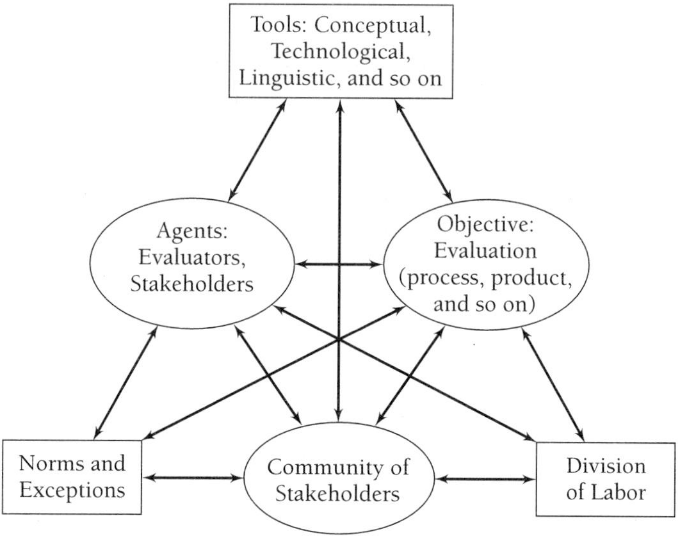

Adapted from Kuutti (1996), p. 28. Used by permission.

reflect on how the situated experiences and demands of evaluation practice mediate evaluators' knowledge production in a dialectical fashion. Like Mark, Henry, and Julnes (1998), we wish here to foreground practice as formative of social programs, knowledge, and values, rather than as simply epiphenomenal to "more fundamental" cognitive components of evaluation (Shadish, Cook, and Leviton, 1991). Evaluators' experiential knowledge, acquired through regular engagement in practical activities, lends evaluation, as a profession and a body of shared knowledge, a uniquely applied character. That knowledge, and the evaluator's consciousness, are further mediated by the tools used, the community of participants in the evaluation project, and the goals of the project.

Object-orientedness (Kaptelinin, 1996, p. 107) in the activity theory model refers to humans' engagement with objects in the world, understood as manifesting a physical integrity independent of their use or users. Activity theorists ascribe objective status not only to physical objects, but also to social and cultural phenomena (Kaptelinin, 1996). This realist position can accommodate anything from naive realism to more nuanced variations of emergent realism (Mark, Henry, and Julnes, 1998). It is premised upon a pragmatic concern with the very real mediating role of tools and technology in human activity, understood as fundamentally oriented toward a world "out there." Artifacts and technologies are used to achieve goals in that world and consequently they transfigure goals and world alike.

Tools, including physical artifacts, symbols, social norms, and conceptual frameworks, mediate among and potentially transform the constituents of an activity as well as the activity itself. As mediators of activities and of learning, tools shape (and are themselves shaped by) consciousness and the social relations in which they are embedded. In the present volume, we are interested in tools in a narrow sense, as electronic technologies and environments, primarily in regards to their mediation of evaluation inquiry. We accomplish evaluative tasks *through* tools—for data collection, analysis, management—and we likewise evaluate the tool use of others, for example, Web-based service delivery or organizations' use of management information systems. Understanding the import of the relationship conveyed by the preposition *through* here is critical; for too often the impact of technologies on our activities is not obvious and remains unaddressed until new technologies appear and provide a basis for comparison. A pertinent example is the differential response rates associated with paper-and-pencil interviewer-administered questionnaires versus various forms of computer-assisted self-administered interviewing and computer-assisted personal interviewing (Tourangeau and Smith, 1996). Activity theory can provide a "clarifying descriptive tool" (Nardi, 1996, p. 7) with which to conceptualize the multiple social variables and technological affordances that affect survey responses, such as the influence of respondents' prior computer experiences, the impact of social norms regarding privacy and confidentiality, degrees of trust in the individuals or groups administering the survey, or the enhancement of an inquiry's credibility that can accrue from the use of computers or new technologies. Tourangeau and Smith found that the mode of data collection affected the reporting of sensitive behaviors such as number of sex partners and illicit drug use.

The activity theory framework prompts us to attend to the relationships and activities technologies enable and to the different places that diverse technologies can potentially take us. This navigational metaphor likewise focuses our attention on the relational function of tools, and forces us to clearly map out the relationship among particular tools, situated contexts of use, and intended destinations. The mediatory and phenomenological metaphors (upon which Nardi and O'Day, 1999, elaborate) enable us to appreciate but also to critically reflect upon the implications of technology use in situated evaluation activities. Where do different tools take us? What do they enable us to accomplish? *How* do they enable us to accomplish tasks or arrive at particular destinations? *How* do they lead our activities down particular epistemological paths or assist our navigation of those paths? How do they simultaneously constitute our direction and destination? Both metaphors draw attention to the significance of social contexts of design and use; both acknowledge and accommodate the non-neutrality of tools and technologies (Ihde, 1990, p. 27).

Technologically Mediated Evaluation: Affordances and Epistemological-Ontological Implications

We can draw upon the activity theory model both to examine how different mediating technologies transform the programs in which they are used (for example, how collaborative groupware is used to facilitate decision making, or how video-based communication tools shape communication in meetings among distant participants), and to reflexively turn our attention to how evaluation practices are themselves transformed through the use of mediating technologies such videotaping, Web-based surveys, or tracking devices. The contributions to this volume discuss tools that potentially enable or enhance the collection, analysis, representation, or dissemination of data in evaluation activities. Because evaluation is an intentional, goal-oriented activity, we can use an activity theory framework to explore the potential uses of each of these tools and their implications for how the objectives of evaluation activities are accomplished. However, it is important to keep in mind that the different motivations, goals, social relations, values, and epistemological frameworks that inform evaluation activities can imply different mediating roles for a tool. That is, if one of the components of an activity changes, then the activity itself potentially becomes a different activity. Shadish, Cook, and Leviton (1991, p. 9) illustrate this differentiation effect when they discuss the different evaluations of a single program that resulted from students' reliance on various theoretical frameworks, which can themselves be conceptualized as cognitive tools.

A tool, such as an on-line survey or a concept, can mediate the social relations, operations, and findings of an evaluation activity differently depending on evaluators' different purposes, approaches, or methods. For example, the use of a Web-based chat room would differ significantly depending upon whether one is conducting a traditional stimulus-response type interview or carrying on a conversation with the purpose of establishing trust and rapport. Likewise, a tool could be designed and used differently by evaluators who perceive the role of evaluator, the "subject" in the above model, as that of "cultural broker" (Fetterman, 1986, p. 22) versus "advocate" (Stake, 1997) versus "objective expert" versus facilitator, or whose motivating objective as evaluator is assessing accountability versus development versus knowledge generation (Chelimsky, 1997, p. 10). As Ihde (1990, p. 128) notes, a "technology is only what it is in some use-context."

Because of the significance of use context in understanding the mediating role of a tool, it is difficult to make generalizations about a tool's efficacy or overall benefit. Whether the use of a tool is to be perceived as a positive or negative contribution to an evaluation depends on the particularities and exigencies of different evaluation use contexts, differing approaches to evaluation, and different situated evaluation activities. More often than not, the introduction of new technologies into a program or activity produces mixed results. For example, the use of multimedia analysis software can provide much richer data to researchers and program participants and can enhance the reliability and validity of qualitative research claims; however, it simultaneously jeopardizes the anonymity and confidentiality of participants (Hesse-Biber, Dupuis, and Kinder, 1997). The increasing reliance of social service providers on electronic record systems has highlighted privacy and confidentiality concerns among social workers recently, concerns also of relevance to evaluators (Gelman, Pollack, and Weiner, 1999). The use of computerized surveys may provide a familiar, relatively nonstressful experience to a youthful evaluation participant but may be anxiety-producing for an older person from a rural area who is unfamiliar and uncomfortable with computers (Beebe and others, 1997). On-line surveys can be cost efficient but still remain useful only for computer-literate populations. With each tool, in each evaluation project, evaluators will have to weigh the significance of these costs and benefits in relation to the project objectives and contexts.

Understanding the affordances, that is, the "perceived and actual properties" (Norman, 1988, p. 9) of objects or tools that shape the possible ways in which they can be used, can facilitate these deliberations. As phenomenologically inspired approaches to technology consistently point out (Ihde, 1990; Heidegger, 1970), any technology simultaneously conceals, reveals, and directs attention and actions in particular ways. Ihde has referred to the "amplification" and "reduction" of human experiences by technology. Heidegger referred to this phenomenon as "enframing." Because technology mediates human-world engagement through disclosing, amplifying, reducing, or enframing realities, and even imputes phenomena with varying degrees of reality, it can imply different epistemological, ontological, theoretical, and methodological positions. Tool use in evaluative inquiry merits critical examination in terms of the concerns raised by activity theory—how are tools selected to meet particular objectives; how do the affordances of a tool shape its use; how do the social, cultural and political contexts affect its use; and what are the implications of a particular tool for the resultant knowledge claims? Several examples within computer-mediated inquiry will help underscore the importance of systematically posing such questions. Computerized qualitative analysis, the increasing reliance on visual data in many forms of research, and the decontextualization inherent in some forms of computer-mediated data collection all illustrate fundamental implications of technologies in use.

Coffey, Holbrook, and Atkinson (1996) and Lonkila (1995) note the emergence of a methodological orthodoxy around the design and use of qualitative data analysis software, particularly through a focus on coding. Coffey, Holbrook, and Atkinson remark that "[t]here is . . . a danger that researchers may be led implicitly towards the uncritical adoption of a particular set of strategies as a consequence of adopting computer-aided analysis." Lonkila notes that through emphasizing "coding" as the primary means of data analysis, the design of software intended for use in qualitative analysis and the management of qualitative data has reinforced "grounded theory" as the preferred approach in the use of such software. She notes that coding draws upon the language of positivistic science via (hypothetico-deductive rhetoric and quantification) and contributes to the devaluation of other types of analysis, such as discourse analysis, rhetorical analysis, narrative analysis, and interpretive approaches more generally. Such a bias, however, can be attenuated through the use of hypertext (illustrating the relevance of the holistic framework provided by activity theory for understanding how and why a particular tool can mediate an activity differently in different contexts). Coffey, Holbrook, and Atkinson note that the hypertext annotations enabled by qualitative analysis software can contribute to more complex, interpretive, and even collaborative analysis and to multiple, contradictory codings and interpretations. The ability to store large quantities of diverse kinds of data, to navigate data via hyperlinks, and to annotate via hypertext can serve to challenge the objectivist bias of coding software. Hence, depending on the use context and the user, analysis software can mediate very different types of analysis and knowledge claims.

A second example of the importance of critically examining tool use involves representational visualization tools, for example, film clips, streaming video, and photographs. Because of the hegemony of visual ways of knowing and presenting knowledge in our society, such tools implicitly privilege naive epistemological assumptions when they present images as unmediated reflections of reality. Such presentations divert attention from their composition, and imply that they depict the world more accurately than other, more obviously constructed, forms of representation. Even visual tools such as cluster maps, graphs, and charts can reduce the complexity and messiness of the real world in such a way as to divert critical attention away from their own rhetorical construction and presentation (Tufte, 1997). As research data and reports become increasingly multimedia, we need to develop more critical literacy skills in order to understand the rhetorical workings of all forms of data representation.

Third, reliance on computer-mediated data collection and analysis can lead to the decontextualization of such data from situated social activities and settings. For example, data derived from tracking devices or cookies, such as those mentioned by Rieger and Sturgill (this volume), can provide detailed records of a computer user's actions or navigation of a website, but cannot provide insight into the contextual and personal factors that give social meaning to those actions. New technologies can make evaluation "from a distance" feasible in terms of ease of data collection and cost; however, the reductionistic implications of such research need to be acknowledged. Even the situated context of the computer-mediated data collection activity itself is complex and merits exploration in order to understand response rates, levels of trust in the medium, emotional responses to technology, and other influential factors. Sheehan and Hoy (1999) illustrate this contextual significance in their attempts to understand respondents' distrust of e-mail administered surveys, stemming in part from respondents' prior experiences with "spamming." Similar complexity characterizes the administration of on-line interviewing, notably the difficulties of "negotiating the ambiguity of the space" of on-line focus groups in the absence of visual clues to meaning (Gaiser, 1997, p. 141).

In short, it behooves evaluators to share their experiences, observations, and reflections upon the use of new technological tools and to engage in a sustained dialogue over their mediating functions and ethical implications before the tools become "transparent" (Ihde, 1990, p. 73). Once new technologies are widely adopted and their use becomes routinized, their mediating role becomes invisible and no longer subject to critical reflection. Those who design technology might desire such transparency, but those professional evaluators who select among technological tools for carrying out applied social inquiry assume a degree of responsibility for the consequences and conditions mediated by their use.

Emergent Technologies and Inquiry Tools

Emergent technologies of particular relevance to evaluation research include multimedia applications for data collection and analysis, the Internet as a tool and environment for research, information systems, tracking tools, and computer-supported collaborative work and learning applications.

Multimedia Applications. Multimedia authoring tools are increasingly available, and numerous software programs have been developed to integrate multiple media into databases for analysis and reporting (see Bennington, Gay, and Jones, this volume). In sociological and anthropological research, especially in ethnography, video has been widely used as a tool for data collection and presentation (Collier and Collier, 1986). As Goldman-Segall notes, digital media are potentially more collaborative and malleable technologies than earlier photographic and filmic media used for data collection (Goldman-Segall, 1998, p. 17). Digital video potentially allows for very fine-grained, rich and thick description, and molecular analysis, supporting evaluation activities motivated by such objectives.

Goldman-Segall has conducted innovative ethnographic research using digital video and multimedia tools for all stages of her research. Her work illustrates the kinds of rich understanding or thick description that digital video can provide and the collaborative, participatory analysis, and "multiloguing" (Goldman-Segall, 1998) that multimedia composition can enable. Nardi and others (1995) also discuss the utility of video as data when integrated into groupware systems, particularly the use of images of workspaces and work objects for evaluating and enhancing task performance. Nardi and others examined the use of live color video to coordinate team activity during neurosurgery and for the remote monitoring of surgical procedures (1995, pp. 208–209). These works illustrate the contributions digital video can make to the activities of documentation and collaboration in social and evaluative inquiry.

However, the use of visual images, including photographs and film, raises numerous epistemological and ontological questions that too often remain unacknowledged. As noted above, the use of video and photography in data collection to "more accurately" represent objective reality contributes to a naive realist position (Harper, 1998). Photographs and film are composed through a process of selection, arrangement, and perspective, features of the medium conducive to more "artistic" forms of evaluation (Eisner, 1991). Ihde (1990, p. 104) aptly summarizes the mediatory relationships entailed in the use of "representational" technologies, noting that "[t]his mirror of life . . . is not isomorphic with nontechnological experience, but is technologically transformed with the various effects that exaggerate or enhance some effects while simultaneously reducing others." Persons and interactions can be photographed or recorded from varying distances, thus fostering differing degrees of intimacy, and background-foreground relationships can emphasize or eliminate contextual features. Not only is the creation of visual images a complex social process, but so is the analysis of images. Because of the limitations of software used for analysis and the typical publication of results in paper form, the analysis and presentation of video data tend to take the form of snapshots, obscuring process and dynamics over time. Goldman-Segall (1998) and Reid and others (1996) draw attention to the ambiguity entailed in the "reading" and analysis of visual data. They conclude that the use of film and photography does not necessarily help resolve contradictions that emerge from other forms of data collection and analysis. Too often inquirers lack a sophisticated understanding of technologies, and hence perceive videotaping as providing authoritative resolution of contradictions among observational data, rather than as offering another perspective. Likewise, photographs and media clips are too often selectively incorporated into findings in order to lend the authority of embodied "presence," in other words, "having been there" to inquirers' claims. As Bennington, Gay, and Jones (this volume) note, integrating multiple media and data effectively requires understanding the limitations as well as advantages of the technologies used, particularly the ways in which different technologies "enframe" the world.

The integration of video and audio data into evaluation practice and reporting, when understood and presented with critical awareness of the aforementioned issues, can enhance validity claims. The incorporation of video and audio segments in multimedia digital reports can lend credence to interpretive knowledge claims, for example, claims regarding the emotional import of an issue to a stakeholder or the quality of interpersonal relations within a program. The emergence of new tools for the annotation, retrieval, and manipulation of video clips and streams facilitates the integration of visual with textual data. Collaborative multimedia tools can also facilitate the participation of diverse stakeholders in multiple stages of the evaluation or in reflective self-evaluation. For example, Hutchinson and Bryson (1997) present the challenges and mixed results that vocational trainers encountered when they attempted to use video both to develop distance training materials and to critically reflect upon and improve their own practice. Digital video can also be distributed to geographically dispersed participants in an evaluation to collaboratively analyze primary data, elicit feedback, and provide checks on evaluators' interpretations (see Bennington, Gay, and Jones, this volume, and Gay, Boehner, and Panella, 1997).

Web-Based Surveys and Evaluation Tools. Increasingly, the Internet provides both context and mediating tools for evaluation research. Web-based surveys provide an inexpensive means of easily reaching targeted populations across the globe (Sheehan and Hoy, 1999; Swoboda, Muehlberger, Weitkunat, and Schneeweiss, 1997; Watt, this volume). Questionnaires and surveys can be administered via e-mail, often to small groups, or via websites to larger national and international groups (Sheehan and Hoy, 1999). However, because of continued, albeit diminishing, unequal access to computers and Internet services, Web-based research is not feasible for many evaluation purposes. The digital delivery of surveys redresses many logistical problems posed by paper-and-pencil methods such as routing problems, skipped questions, inconsistent responses, and interviewer inconsistencies; digital surveys facilitate the customization of questions and the incorporation of visual stimuli. In this volume Watt and Rieger and Sturgill describe the process of collecting such data via the Internet and raise in greater detail the concomitant methodological and logistical advantages and challenges posed by using cyberspace as a research tool and environment.

"Distanced" evaluation activity poses new methodological challenges and requires transforming practices to accommodate distance relationships and communication. Group communication needs to be facilitated differently in the absence of embodied expression, cooperation enlisted differently, and confidentiality and anonymity (if guaranteed) protected differently. (See Finn, Sellen, and Wilbur, 1997, for discussions of some of the communicative effects of "remoteness"; see Gaiser, 1997, on on-line focus groups.) Evaluators conducting interviews or observing on-line discussions need to understand how various aspects of communication are constricted or enhanced through different tools; for example, asynchronous exchanges may foster more reflective engagement but may not reveal immediate emotional responses to issues. Moreover, responses are significantly shaped by participants' writing skills and levels of comfort with communicating through a particular communication medium (see Gotcher and Kanervo, 1997, for a discussion of e-mail). Tools that enable evaluation from a geographical or temporal distance also foster different types of relationships and engagement among stakeholders with potential methodological and ethical implications, addressed by Bennington in the conclusion to this volume.

Again, returning to the activity theory model, whether and how these different forms of "distance" mediate an evaluation activity is contingent upon the tools used, the goals of the activity, the commitments of the evaluator, and the social context. For example, evaluation for the purpose of accountability can be understood as premised upon a relatively distanced relationship between the evaluator and the evaluand; the use of "distance" technologies and "distanced" relationships might therefore be more compatible with such an activity than with a participatory project. Or, as Nardi and others (1995) demonstrate, distanced engagement can prove a more effective means of accomplishing some tasks than embodied presence. For example, listening to and observing neurosurgery is easier and more focused from a location distant from the diverse aural and visual stimuli of the operating room. Such findings challenge commonsense notions of remoteness and presence, providing an example of what Nardi and others (1995, p. 217) refer to, following Hollan and Stornetta (1992), as "beyond being there," where "being remote is preferable to being co-located."

Information Systems. Information systems designed for the collection and organization of information for monitoring, evaluating, and learning also mediate program and evaluation activities in ways that merit reflection. Savaya (1998) discusses the use of an integrated information system to evaluate the process and outcomes of treatment interventions in a family and marriage counseling agency. Information systems, when appropriately designed to compile, analyze, and represent program information, can become tools for a program's self-monitoring and learning and can facilitate formative evaluation. Savaya (1998, p. 15) illustrates how an information system can "serve as a foundation for empirically based practice" when it is designed to fit an agency's particular needs. Again, the information management system was effective because of the appropriate "fit" among the tool, the objectives of the agents, and the local social context. Shum (1998, p. 76) enumerates the relevant design issues for such a system if it is to be used for formative evaluation as well as for a program's data collection and management; for example, the need to determine which classes of knowledge or expertise are to be addressed by these systems, how information is to be represented, what kinds of analyses are enabled by those representations, and how the system will impact the work of stakeholders. Understanding these design and use issues is critical for evaluating the systems themselves as well as the meanings and significance of the information they collect and store and how they mediate organizational practices and decision making.

Other information systems can facilitate the evaluation of programs and service delivery, such as health care. Plaisant, Shneiderman, and Mushlin (1998) summarize their work with LifeLines, an information architecture for visualizing personal histories. Hospitalizations, consultations, and other life events of relevance to an individual's health and medical treatment can be visually mapped onto juxtaposed time lines, thus enabling health care providers and evaluators see at a glance the relationships among these elements of an individual's history and the treatment and services they have received. The information provided by such a system could facilitate formative and summative evaluation in the diverse programs using it by providing concise, meaningful information in a readily accessible visual form that can be hyperlinked to evaluation data, interpretations, and discussions. Geographic information systems, by mapping demographic data onto geographical representations, can provide similar useful visual data for evaluators assessing issues of distribution and distributive justice (Tompkins and Southward, 1998). Tompkins and Southward advocate the integration of Geographic Information Systems (GIS) into social work in order to facilitate the evaluation of services, research, and teaching. They illustrate how researchers with the Social Science Research Council can interactively and non-interactively use GIS technology to visualize data and how it can be used to facilitate policymaking in child welfare services and jobs programs.

Electronic Tracking Tools. Rieger and Sturgill in this volume provide an overview of different tracking devices and how they can be used as an unobtrusive means of collecting data to evaluate the efficiency or usability of computer-delivered programs. Such tools can contribute to richly descriptive evaluations; for example, to assessing whether and how an electronic collaborative work environment contributed to decision making and policymaking processes or how a user navigates a website to find information or use the services provided through the website. Tracking, through applications such as ScreenCam, can supplement interview data relating the perceived use of these technologies with detailed data that document actual use. Both the Rieger and Sturgill and Bennington, Gay, and Jones chapters in this volume enumerate the benefits of such technologies for evaluation inquiry.

However, such unobtrusive but potentially invasive technologies raise numerous concerns regarding surveillance, "dataveillance," confidentiality, privacy, anonymity, and informed consent. They potentially threaten multiple trust relationships; for example, when tracking devices are used to monitor employee performance or productivity. Even monitoring how users navigate a site or use information resources (for example, a library catalog) while maintaining anonymity can violate users' expectations of privacy and anonymity when they are unaware that their actions are being recorded. In fact, tracking tools raise serious legal and ethical questions about the nature of privacy and even the distinction between public and private (Jones, 1994), as do many emerging technologies.

Computer-Supported Collaborative Work and Communication Applications. Other tools with transformative implications for evaluation activities include computer-supported collaborative work tools such as Lotus Notes, RepTool, Folio Views, and Trochim's concept-mapping package. All of these tools can be used to facilitate interaction, communication, and collaboration among members of work teams, among diverse organizational personnel, and among evaluators and other stakeholders.

RepTool was designed by the Institute for Research on Learning and Bell Atlantic for the collection, management, and analysis of information related to "workscapes." It enables users to collaboratively map the physical layout of work spaces, social relationships and networks, and technological infrastructure, and to use the mappings to facilitate evaluation and learning. Depending on one's theoretical orientation and the particular type of evaluation one is conducting, such a collaborative tool can support participatory inquiry, detailed descriptive evaluation, or variations of network analysis. The capacity to visually represent workflow and patterns of interaction, mapping them onto layouts of physical work settings, can facilitate the identification of potentially significant relationships.

Trochim's (Computer Systems Incorporated) concept-mapping program is another tool that enables active participation of stakeholders in evaluation activities through brain-storming and the visual representation of concepts and categories elicited from a group. Through multidimensional scaling and cluster analysis the program maps relationships among the concepts. It is a powerful tool for "disclosing" the existence and interconnections of ideas within a group and can be used with interviewing, in an integrated mixed-method design (Caracelli and Greene, 1997), or to facilitate decision making, strategic planning, and other activities often associated with formative evaluation and learning.

Groupware applications that are already established in programs or organizations for the management of information and for collaborative work and learning, such as LotusNotes, can provide invaluable textual data for use in evaluations as well as a forum for the collaborative activities of evaluators and program stakeholders. These collaborative groupware applications can facilitate input and feedback from stakeholders. In a more radical form, they could be used in transformative participatory evaluation (Cousins and Whitmore, 1998) to enable participants to actively engage in all stages of the evaluation process, from initial design to the creation and dissemination of findings. Participation can be facilitated when participants use a groupware tool with which they are already familiar. The conceptual framework of activity theory helps us identify the more systemic social and normative relations in which such technologies function and the practical activities they mediate and transform.

Groupware applications enable participation and collaboration among not only geographically dispersed individuals and groups but also among stakeholders who cannot be present for face-to-face meetings. They can also provide alternative forms of group interaction that, if moderated appropriately, can reduce some of the effects of social status and power inequalities that can negatively affect focus group and interviewer-interviewee relations. Such applications should not be seen as a substitute for face-to-face interaction but as a supplement that can address the shortcomings of other methods, including face-to-face engagement. Again, computer-supported collaborative work applications potentially enable and facilitate participatory and empowerment evaluation through providing applications that allow diverse stakeholders to be actively involved in all stages of the evaluation process, from design to the interpretation and dissemination of findings. Moreover, they can provide these same supports for evaluation activities themselves.

Points for Sustained Reflection

As noted above, activity theory cautions us that the use of any tool potentially transforms the activity in which it is used and, reciprocally, tools are transformed in the process of their use. A tool must be selected with consideration of the objectives motivating its use and the social contexts in which it will be used. Responsible evaluation professionals need to document and critically analyze situated uses of technology in both program settings and evaluation inquiries so as to understand the mediating functions of different technologies and tools or, to paraphrase Nardi and O'Day (1999), to thoughtfully engage with technologies as they are used in local habitations.

We would like to offer, drawing upon the activity theory model presented above, a number of recommendations for the reflective and responsible evaluation of technology use in evaluation habitations, as well as in computer-mediated program delivery. Issues meriting sustained exploration include the following:

- Is there compatibility, or local coherence, among the technology, methods, and objectives of the evaluation? For example, will using a self-administered Web-based survey enhance response rates regarding sensitive behaviors?
- Is there compatibility among a tool or technology, the theoretical orientation of the researcher, and the evaluation context? Is the tool, in terms of its affordances, compatible with the ontological premises of the evaluation? For example, will a particular collaborative groupware application be accessible to all stakeholders and afford their equitable participation in a participatory, empowerment evaluation project?
- What are the epistemological implications, as well as justifications for the use of a particular tool? For example, is the use of visual images to collect data premised upon naive realist representational assumptions?
- How does the technology fit with the community's existing social norms, practices, and past experiences with technology? For example, does the use of a self-administered computer-based survey provide an uncomfortable or alienating experience for some participants because of their lack of experience with computer technology?
- Does the technology enable or facilitate the participation of diverse stakeholders or a broader community of practitioners? For example, do all participants have access to the results of evaluations that are disseminated through e-mail or through the Internet? Similarly, how many human service providers have access to the databases and information that are increasingly available via Internet fora such as websites, e-mail, bulletin boards, and chat rooms (Giffords, 1998)?
- Does the technology or tool enable the collection of data in a manner that facilitates learning, improved decision making, or reflective practice? Does

it thereby transform extant practices and relations? Does the technology or tool potentially contribute to formative or summative evaluation?

- What are the social implications of the technology in diverse use contexts; for example, is the technology or tool designed to enable or foster collaboration and communication among multiple participants, or does it require a centralized or top-down implementation? How does the successful use of the tool, for example, a collaborative work application, depend on particular group norms or coordinated practices?
- Should diverse stakeholders be involved in decision making regarding the use of the technology and, if so, how? Many technologies, such as information management systems and collaborative groupware applications, can facilitate collective decision making at all stages of the evaluation inquiry.
- What are the ethical implications of the technology in diverse use contexts? For example, does a tracking device potentially compromise users' expectations of privacy or anonymity?
- What are the relevant usability issues, that is, is the technology easy to use? Is it accessible to a large number of stakeholders in the evaluation, or to only a select few? Does it limit possible forms of communication, for example, to asynchronous written exchanges, which may exclude participants with poor written communication skills?
- What evaluation practices are transformed or displaced by implementation and use of the technology? For example, what are the multiple consequences of replacing face-to-face interviews with video conferencing?

Professionally responsible use of new technologies necessitates addressing these issues. Too often such considerations are accorded the selection of methods, but not necessarily the selection research technologies. As Shadish, Cook, and Leviton (1991, p. 61) have noted, "Practice is about making constrained choices with a realistic understanding of losses and gains." In the technologically textured world of evaluation, it behooves evaluators to systematically evaluate the mediating role of technologies in evaluation activities themselves. The remainder of chapters in this volume will provide such reflections.

References

Beebe, T. J., Mika, T., Harrison, P. A., Anderson, R. E., and Fulkerson, J. A. "Computerized School Surveys." *Social Science Computer Review*, 1997, 5 (2), 159–169.

Bellamy, R. K. E. "Designing Educational Technology: Computer-Mediated Change." In B. A. Nardi (ed.), *Context and Consciousness: Activity Theory and Human-Computer Interaction*. Cambridge, Mass., and London: MIT Press, 1996.

Caracelli, V. J., and Greene, J. C. "Crafting Mixed-Method Evaluation Designs." In J. C. Greene and V. J. Caracelli (eds.), *Advances in Mixed-Method Evaluation: The Challenges and Benefits of Integrating Diverse Paradigms*. New Directions for Evaluation, no. 74. San Francisco: Jossey-Bass, 1997.

Chelimsky, E. "The Coming Transformations in Evaluation." In E. Chelimsky and W. Shadish (eds.), *Evaluation for the 21st Century: A Handbook*. Thousand Oaks: Sage, 1997.

Coffey, A., Holbrook. B., and Atkinson. P. "Qualitative Data Analysis: Technologies and Representation." *Sociological Research Online*, 1996, 1 (1). [http://www.socresonline.org.uk/socresonline/1/1/4.html]

Collier, J. J., and Collier, M. *Visual Anthropology: Photography as a Research Method.* Albuquerque: University of New Mexico Press, 1986.

Cousins, J. B., and Whitmore, E. "Framing Participatory Evaluation." In E. Whitmore (ed.), *Understanding and Practicing Participatory Evaluation.* New Directions for Evaluation, no. 80. San Francisco: Jossey-Bass, 1998.

Eisner, E. W. *The Enlightened Eye: Qualitative Inquiry and the Enhancement of Educational Practice.* New York, Macmillan, 1991.

Fetterman, D. M. "The Ethnographic Evaluator." In D. M. Fetterman and M. A. Pitman (eds.), *Educational Evaluation: Ethnography in Theory, Practice, and Politics.* Beverly Hills: Sage, 1986.

Fetterman, D. M., Kaftarian, S. J., and Wandersman, A. *Empowerment Evaluation: Knowledge and Tools for Self-Assessment and Accountability.* Thousand Oaks, Calif.: Sage, 1996.

Finn, K. E., Sellen, A. J., and Wilbur, S. B. (eds.) *Video-Mediated Communication.* Mahwah, N.J.: Erlbaum, 1997.

Gaiser, T. J. "Conducting On-Line Focus Groups: A Methodological Discussion." *Social Science Computer Review*, 1997, 15 (2), 135–144.

Gay, G., Boehner, K., and Panella, T. "ArtView: Transforming Image Databases into Collaborative Learning Spaces." *Journal of Educational Computing Research*, 1997, 16 (4), 317–332.

Gelman, S. R., Pollack, D., and Weiner, A. "Confidentiality of Social Work Records in the Computer Age." *Social Work*, 1999, 44(3), 243–252.

Giffords, E. D. "Social Work on the Internet: An Introduction." *Social Work*, 1998, 43 (3), 243–251.

Goldman-Segall, R. *Points of Viewing Children's Thinking: A Digital Ethnographer's Journey.* Mahwah, N.J.: Erlbaum, 1998.

Gotcher, J. M., and Kanervo, E. W. "Perceptions and Uses of Electronic Mail: A Function of Rhetorical Style." *Social Science Computer Review*, 1997, 15 (2), 145–158.

Harper, D. "On the Authority of the Image: Visual Methods at the Crossroads." In N. Denzin and Y. Lincoln (eds.), *Collecting and Interpreting Qualitative Materials.* Thousand Oaks, Calif.: Sage Publications, 1998.

Heidegger, M. *The Question Concerning Technology and Other Essays.* New York: Harper & Row, 1970.

Hesse-Biber, S., Dupuis, P. R., and Kinder, T. S. "Anthropology: New Developments in Video Ethnography and Visual Sociology—Analyzing Multimedia Data Qualitatively." *Social Science Computer Review*, 1997, 15 (1):5–12.

Hollan, J., and Stornetta, S. "Beyond Being There." *Proceedings Computer-Human Interaction '92.* New York: Association of Computing Machinery, 1992, pp. 119–125.

Hutchinson, B., and Bryson, P. "Video, Reflection and Transformation: Action Research in Vocational Education and Training in a European Context." *Educational Action Research*, 1997, 5 (2), 283–303.

Ihde, D. *Technology and the Lifeworld: From Garden to Eden.* Bloomington and Indianapolis: Indiana University Press, 1990.

Jones, R. A. "The Ethics of Research in Cyberspace." *Internet Research*, 1994, 4 (3), 30–35.

Kaptelinin, V. "Activity Theory: Implications for Human-Computer Interaction." In B. A. Nardi (ed.), *Context and Consciousness: Activity Theory and Human-Computer Interaction.* Campbridge, Mass and London: MIT Press, 1996.

Kilker, J., and Gay, G. "The Social Construction of a Digital Library: A Case Study Examining Implications for Evaluation." *Information Technology and Libraries*, 1998, 17 (2), 60–69.

Kuutti, K. "Activity Theory as a Potential Framework for Human-Computer Interaction Research." In B. A. Nardi (ed.), *Context and Consciousness: Activity Theory and Human-Computer Interaction.* Cambridge, Mass., and London: MIT Press, 1996.

Lonkila, M. "Grounded Theory as an Emerging Paradigm for Computer-Assisted Qualitative Data Analysis." In U. Kelle (ed.), *Computer-Aided Qualitative Data Analysis.* London: Sage, 1995.

Mark, M. M., Henry, G. T., and Julnes, G. "A Realist Theory of Evaluation Practice." In G. Henry, G. Julnes, and M. Mark (eds.), *Realist Evaluation: An Emerging Theory in Support of Practice.* New Directions for Evaluation, no.78. San Francisco: Jossey-Bass, 1998.

Mead, J. P., and Gay, G. "Concept Mapping: An Innovative Approach to Digital Library Design and Evaluation." Proceedings of the 37th Allerton Institute, University of Illinois, Champaign-Urbana, 1995. [http://edfu.lis.uiuc.edu/allerton/95/s2/mead/mead.html]

Nardi, B. A. "Activity Theory and Human-Computer Interaction." In B. A. Nardi (ed.), *Context and Consciousness: Activity Theory and Human-Computer Interaction.* Cambridge, Mass., and London: MIT Press, 1996.

Nardi, B. A., and O'Day, V. L. *Information Ecologies: Using Technology with Heart.* Cambridge, Mass., and London: MIT Press, 1999.

Nardi, B., Schwarz, H., Kuchinsky, A., Leichner, R., Whittaker, S., and Sclabassi, R. "Turning Away from Talking Heads: Video-as-Data in Neurosurgery." In S. Emmott (ed.), *Information Superhighways: Multimedia Users and Futures.* London and New York: Academic Press, 1995.

Norman, D. *The Psychology of Everyday Things.* New York: Basic Books, 1988.

Plaisant, C., Shneiderman, B., and Mushlin, R. "An Information Architecture to Support the Visualization of Personal Histories." *Information Processing and Management,* 1998, *34* (5), 581–597.

Reid, J., Kamler, B., Simpson, A., and MacLean, R. "'Do You See What I See?' Reading a Different Classroom Scene." *Qualitative Studies in Education,* 1996, *9* (1), 87–107.

Savaya, R. "The Potential and Utilization of an Integrated Information System at a Family and Marriage Counseling Agency in Israel." *Evaluation and Program Planning,* 1998, *21,* 11–20.

Shadish, W. R., Cook, T. D., and Leviton, L. C. *Foundations of Program Evaluation: Theory of Practice.* Newbury Park, Calif.: Sage, 1991.

Sheehan, K. B., and Hoy, M. G. "Using E-mail to Survey Internet Users in the United States: Methodology and Assessment." *Journal of Computer Mediated Communication,* 1999, *4* (3). [http://www.ascusc.org/jcmc/vol4/issue3/sheehan.html]

Shum, S. B. "Negotiating the Construction of Organisational Memories." In U. Borghoff and R. Pareschi (eds.), *Information Technology for Knowledge Management.* Berlin: Springer-Verlag, 1998.

Stake, R. E. "Advocacy in Evaluation: A Necessary Evil?" In E. Chelimsky and W. Shadish (eds.), *Evaluation for the 21st Century: A Handbook.* Thousand Oaks, Calif.: Sage, 1997.

Swoboda, W. J., Muehlberger, N., Weitkunat, R., and Schneeweiss, S. "Internet Surveys by Direct Mailing: An Innovative Way of Collecting Data." *Social Science Computer Review* 1997, *15* (3), 242–255.

Tompkins, P. L., and Southward, L. H. "Geographic Information Systems (GIS): Implications for Promoting Social and Economic Justice." *Computers in Human Services,* 1998, *5* (2/3), 209–226.

Tourangeau, R., and Smith, T. W. "Asking Sensitive Questions: The Impact of Data Collection Mode, Question Format, and Question Context." *Public Opinion Quarterly,* 1996, *60,* 275–304.

Trochim, W. M. K. "An Introduction to Concept Mapping for Planning and Evaluation." n.d. [http://trochim.human.cornell.edu/research/epp1/epp1.htm]

Tufte, E. *Visual Explanations: Images and Quantities, Evidence and Narrative.* Cheshire, Conn.: Graphics Press, 1997.

GERI GAY is associate professor in the department of communications at Cornell University and director of the Human-Computer Interaction Group at Cornell.

TAMMY L. BENNINGTON is research associate in the Human-Computer Interaction Group at Cornell University and adjunct professor in the Program on Social and Organizational Learning at George Mason University.

2

The author provides a detailed description of diverse Web-based data collection tools and enumerates their advantages, disadvantages, and logistical challenges. Web-based data collection can offer cost-effective, flexible, and timely solutions to many evaluation needs.

Internet Systems for Evaluation Research

James H. Watt

Many evaluation projects require data collection in either questionnaire form or from personal interviews or group discussions. For many projects, these data are increasingly expensive and difficult to obtain with traditional methods. Survey research costs are steep (Watt, 1997), and respondent cooperation with interviewers is decreasing. Focus group facilitators and professional moderators and interviewers are also very expensive.

The Internet provides a partial answer to these problems for some data collection needs. On-line data collection can be used as a supplement to traditional methods of collecting information or as a replacement for these methods (Bertot and McClure, 1996; Fulop, 1997; Persichitte, 1997). Certain kinds of studies, such as responses to detailed audio-visual demonstrations, can be conducted via Internet when they are not feasible with other methods. Even as a simple replacement for traditional methods, Internet data collection provides some significant advantages in cost, flexibility, and the speed with which data can be obtained.

Successful use of the Internet for evaluation research depends upon the proper conjunction of three factors: the technologies available, the inquiry question, and the population being studied. The interrelationships of these factors are the focus of this chapter.

Different Methods of Conducting Internet Data Collection

The Internet can be used asynchronously or synchronously to collect data. Asynchronous data collection does not require the evaluator or interviewer to be on-line or directly connected to the respondent at the time the information is provided by the respondent. An example is an e-mail questionnaire that can be filled out and returned at any time by the respondent. Synchronous data collection is used when more immediate interactive communication with the respondent is desired. An example is a focus group conducted in a real-time Web chat room. Table 2.1 illustrates some methods for gathering data on the Internet. The methods use questionnaires or discussion transcripts as the basic technique for data collection.

E-mail Questionnaires. The questionnaire is prepared like a simple e-mail message, and is sent to a list of known e-mail addresses. The respondent fills in the answers, and e-mails the form plus replies back to the evaluation organization. A computer program is often used to prepare the questionnaire, the e-mail address list, and to extract the data from the replies.

Advantages. E-mail questionnaires are simple to construct and fast to distribute. By showing up in the respondent's e-mailbox, they demand immediate attention.

Disadvantages. E-mail questionnaires are generally limited to plain text, although graphics might be sent as e-mail attachments that are decoded separately from the questionnaire text. Many standard questionnaire layout techniques, such as creating grids of questions and scale responses, cannot be done in a visually attractive way in e-mail. There is no check for validity of data until the whole questionnaire is returned, so there is no opportunity to request that the respondent reenter bad data. The respondent may damage the questionnaire text in the process of responding, thereby making automatic data extraction impossible and requiring hand coding of damaged responses. In addition, all logical question skips are carried out by the respondent, who is given a set of instructions embedded in the text ("If you replied 'yes' to this question, skip to Question 23"). This can result in illegal skip patterns, which may require hand recoding, or may result in missing data or rejected questionnaires.

Web Common Gateway Interface (CGI) Programs. In this approach to Internet data collection, each questionnaire is programmed directly in html (HyperText Markup Language, the presentation language used by Web

Table 2.1. Internet Data Collection Methods

	Synchronous	Asynchronous
Questionnaires		E-mail
		Web CGI programs
		Web survey systems
Transcripts	One-on-one text interview	Web focus groups via text conferencing
	One-on-one A/V interview	One-on-one interviews via e-mail
	Web focus groups via chat	
	Web focus groups via A/V	

browsers) by using a computer script language such as PERL or a programming language such as Visual Basic. The programmed questionnaire is placed on a Web server at the client's location or on a server located in a service bureau. The program uses the Common Gateway Interface (CGI) in html to receive respondents' replies and a program to place them into a database. Database queries can be programmed to give periodic reports of the data, including statistical analyses.

Advantages. The CGI programming approach is very flexible. Complex question skips and data verification and reentry can be achieved, and programming languages can use the full capability of the Web. Since all questionnaires are custom programmed, Web CGI programs are not tied to a proprietary computer or application language, or to a single technology vendor. Database operations and queries can be programmed to adapt to virtually any special reporting need of the researcher.

Disadvantages. This flexibility comes with a cost, however. Since questionnaires and their database operations are realized in custom computer programs that must be created and debugged by highly trained programmers, they are expensive. The computer languages contain no special tools for tasks such as respondent screening, sample quota management, and question skip pattern management, so programming these features in each questionnaire further increases the cost.

The CGI program must be placed on a Web server system to distribute the questionnaires and collect the data. This can be the evaluation client's Web server, or a server provided by the evaluator. If the survey is placed on the client's Web server, time for programming and debugging can be difficult to schedule. Large sites often require several administrative approvals before any modifications of the site can be made, and technical staff members are frequently leery of allowing an outside programmer to place a program on their site.

Web Survey Systems. These are software systems specifically designed for Web questionnaire construction and delivery. In essence, they combine the survey administration tools of a CATI (Computer Aided Telephone Interviewing) system with the flexibility of CGI programming. CATI-like tools include automatic sampling quota management, integrated mail, and e-mail recruiting tools. Automated personalization of the questionnaire can be provided with some Web survey systems, a feature traditionally found to be important in improving the respondent cooperation rate (Dillman, 1991). Web survey systems typically consist of an integrated questionnaire designer, Web server, database, and data delivery program, all designed for use by nonprogrammers.

In a typical use, the questionnaire is constructed with an easy-to-use questionnaire editor using a visual interface, then automatically transmitted to a Web server system maintained by the Web survey service provider. The Web server distributes the questionnaire to respondents and files their responses in a database. The user can query the server at any time via the

Web for completion statistics, descriptive statistics on responses, and graphical displays of data. Data can be downloaded from the server for analysis at the researcher's location. The questionnaire construction and data display programs reside on the user's computer system, while the Web server is located in the survey technology provider's office.

Advantages. Web survey systems include tools that allow nonprogrammers to create complex questionnaires that are visually appealing. The complexity of skip patterns and data verification that can be achieved is similar to CGI programming. Users do not have to maintain a website or database, so there is less disruption of clients' websites and computing facilities. Sample quota control is very good. In addition, tools to personalize questionnaires with database information (such as inserting the respondent's name or organizational information in an evaluation questionnaire delivered to a sample respondent) and to add graphics and sound without programming are often big pluses. For example, evaluations of individuals' job performance can include samples of their work in text, visual, or video form, directly attached to the Web questionnaire. Product concept evaluations can include a demonstration of a hypothetical product, prior to soliciting questionnaire responses. For complicated evaluation procedures, a video "training session" can be attached to the questionnaire.

Web survey systems typically have a lower cost per completed interview than CGI programs, although they are more expensive than e-mail surveys for surveys under 1,000 respondents. For very large surveys, they are the cheapest method. For example, for 10,000 respondents, a typical cost per respondent for a Web survey is $0.65, whereas an e-mail survey's cost for a similar survey is $1.64 (costs are discussed in detail in the next section). The lower cost results from the efficiencies of using software tools designed specifically for Web use, and from the cost-sharing of Internet access charges and computer hardware that a central server system provides.

Disadvantages. Like CGI programming, Web survey systems use the more passive Web retrieval for questionnaires. E-mail, although it has many limitations, is more immediately attention-demanding. Some Web survey systems integrate e-mail recruitment and reminders to partially address this problem. Web survey systems, although designed for nonprogrammers, still have a learning curve that makes them more economical for repeated professional use than for a single isolated survey.

One-on-One Text-Based Internet Interviews. Text-based systems can be used by an interviewer to collect information synchronously from a single respondent. One common method uses instant-message software on the interviewer's and respondent's computers. Each copy of the messaging software has a unique ID, so that any two people can connect their computers by knowing each other's ID. The interviewer and respondent interact by typing questions and answers in a text area that is viewed by both parties. The interview is conducted in a standard back-and-forth manner.

A variation uses a synchronous chat system. In this system, respondents and the moderator connect to a server system via the Internet. This system provides "chat rooms" or areas for interaction. These can be set up to require a password, so that unauthorized access to the discussion is prohibited. The respondent and the moderator type questions and comments in a text area that is seen by both.

Advantages. Text-based interviews via Internet eliminate interviewer travel expenses, which can be a major cost of this kind of data collection. They also provide an instant transcript with no transcribing cost, as the messaging or chat software can be instructed to save and print the text interaction.

Disadvantages. The major disadvantage is the lack of face-to-face contact and the loss of nonverbal visual or vocal information, as compared to in-person or telephone interviews. The speed with which the interview proceeds is also much slower than in-person or telephone interviews. Another major disadvantage is the requirement that all respondents have compatible chat or message software installed on their computer systems. Although client systems are freely available for download on the Internet, different systems are often incompatible with each other. This situation differs markedly from that of Web browsers, which are essentially interchangeable and much more widely distributed and installed than are messaging or chat software.

One-on-One Audio-Visual Internet Interviews. In this situation, the interviewer and respondent have installed on their computers a videophone system that includes a small camera and a microphone. The interview is conducted essentially as a videoconference. This kind of interview requires more installed computer hardware and software than a text-based interview, and for that reason is much less frequently used.

Advantages. The nonverbal information of the interaction is captured. It may be recorded on videotape by the interviewer for later analysis. The speed of the interview approximates normal conversation, so the interaction is closer to that which would occur face to face.

Disadvantages. Audio-visual systems require a fairly high-speed Internet connection for even minimal quality audio and video. Internet connections via modems are almost always unacceptable for audio-visual sessions, as the video frames are refreshed at such a slow rate that they are more a distraction than a source of information. With slow modem connections, the audio frequently pauses and is sometimes lost. In addition, a written transcript must be produced at extra expense at a later time.

Web Focus Groups. A Web focus group duplicates some of the moderated group interaction of a traditional face-to-face focus group discussion. Web focus groups can be conducted with text interaction (the most common method) or by using the audio-visual capabilities of the Internet.

Text-Based Focus Groups. These groups can use a variety of different conferencing tools. A simple method uses a synchronous chat system that works like the one-on-one system described above, except that more than two participants are connected by the server. The respondents and the moderator type questions and comments in an area on the screen, and every member of the group sees the comments of all other members.

Text-based Web focus groups can also be conducted asynchronously by using computer conferencing tools. The simplest form of asynchronous conferencing tool is the e-mail list server. Participants in a focus group using this tool e-mail their comments and reactions to the list, and all members of the list receive the material in their e-mail.

More sophisticated conferencing software can be used to conduct asynchronous group discussions. This software typically supports "threaded" discussions, that is, discussions that are arranged by topic. A moderator often sets up the initial discussion threads, and the participants attach text messages to each thread, thereby responding to the questions and statements of the moderator and other group members. Group participants may or may not be allowed to start new threads, depending on the degree of control that the discussion moderator desires. When participants log onto the group conferencing server, they are typically directed to the threads that have been most active recently. Participants can read and post messages on a number of threads in one session, thus taking part in a discussion of several different topics.

Advantages. Chat or list server focus groups use very inexpensive software that is widely available. Almost all Internet users have e-mail software to participate in list server groups, and many potential respondents already have chat client software installed. Chat server software can be downloaded from many Internet sources. Text chat groups can involve respondents who have slow Internet connections, as text interaction requires a very low bandwidth.

Disadvantages. The speed of text synchronous group interaction is limited to typing speed, and this limitation alters the group interaction (Baym, 1995). Synchronous text-based Web focus groups produce discussions that differ markedly from those produced in face-to-face situations. For tightly focused discussions, this may not be a drawback and in fact may be an advantage. Some respondents in task-oriented Web text focus groups have commented that the additional time to think and type in asynchronous groups improves the quality and succinctness of their comments. But for groups that need a more free-wheeling discussion, text-based groups may be inhibiting.

Synchronous communication produces results from group discussion that are closer to face-to-face results than does asynchronous communication. However, the results of text-based synchronous focus groups are still distinctly different from those obtained from face-to-face groups. It is not valid to compare the two directly. Internet focus groups, and particularly text-based groups, are better seen as a different method of research, rather than as an equivalent of face-to-face groups. Interpretation of transcripts must take into account the linear nature of the discussion, the more limited opportunities for interruption and interjection, and the lack of nonverbal feedback to the moderator.

Asynchronous list server discussions are very slow to evolve, since responses to queries or comments are often delayed a day or two. Discussions tend to focus very linearly on one discussion item at a time in "comment-response-response to the response" sequence, so they tend to produce fairly simple discussions. List server group discussions are most successful when a very narrow topic is defined, and group members are knowledgeable about the topic. In this case, the focus and linearity of discussion is not a liability.

Threaded discussions can handle more complex topics, but can result in a scattered focus. Participants may choose to participate in discussion of only a few topics, and discussion threads may die off when "hotter" topics are introduced. The natural flow from one topic to a related topic is also missing, and the discussion may proceed as a series of only loosely related fragments.

Both asynchronous methods (list server and threaded conference group discussion) differ from synchronous one-on-one and chat group discussions. The comments and responses are composed like e-mail messages, and often appear to be much less spontaneous than synchronous discussion. However, the detail and logical structure of the responses in an asynchronous group discussion are generally superior to those in synchronous groups.

It is harder to keep participants' attention and motivation levels high in both forms of asynchronous text discussion, since the social pressure to respond and contribute to the discussion that is present in synchronous discussions is missing. Threaded conferencing software typically requires that the participant log onto the server, that is, that the participant make a special effort to participate in the discussion. Some conferencing software sends daily e-mail reminders with some indication of recent discussion activity in order to create a motivation to log on and participate further in group discussions.

Audio, Visual, and Mixed Media Focus Groups. These groups use some combination of advanced electronic communication tools, often combining asynchronous text discussions with synchronous audio-visual teleconferences. Group participants see and hear each other during synchronous discussions. Other tools, such as a common drawing area (*whiteboard*), a document repository, and multiple-user text editors, may be available, as well. The moderator may direct group participants to look at audio-visual presentations and/or read text documents, then return to an audio-visual chat room for the group discussion. Synchronous discussions may be combined with later asynchronous text-based discussion.

Advantages. This is the richest, most capable environment for group interaction. The availability of different communication tools and modes of communication is very well suited to discussion of complex situations that may require supporting materials. The environment combines the advantages of asynchronous and synchronous groups, and can combine interviews with questionnaire responses. The real-time audio-visual environment allows synchronous group discussion moderators to employ the standard skill set of the focus group moderator: sensitive reaction to nonverbal cues, detailed probing, and so on. The transcripts that result are more like those from face-to-face discussions, although the mediating technology still introduces significant differences in participant and moderator interactions.

Disadvantages. Software to support these groups is large, expensive, and unstandardized. The group participants need fairly advanced computer skills to operate the various communication tools. As for one-on-one audio-visual interviewing, participant connections must be relatively high-speed. In general, this type of group can only be conducted in organizations that have already installed standardized software packages for group interaction or collaborative work, often within their own private high-speed network!

Costs of Traditional and Internet Data Collection Methods

Figures 2.1 and 2.2 illustrate a major advantage of Internet research for both synchronous and asynchronous data collection. In general, it is cheaper to collect data using the Internet than it is with traditional methods, especially if the size of the sample is relatively large. The costs in these figures were obtained from commercial research firms, and reflect the full cost of data collection, including interviewer salaries, data handling and entry costs, mailing, travel, focus group facility fees, interview and group discussion transcript preparation, and overhead.

For questionnaires, the costs shown in these figures are based on an eight–page questionnaire that can be administered via telephone in approximately twelve minutes. The mail questionnaire response rate is assumed to be 25 percent and the cooperation rate with telephone interviewing is 50 percent. For focus group and in-person interviews, the costs are based on a one–hour interview or discussion, with daily travel costs for the moderator or interviewer. Focus groups have an assumed size of eight participants.

Of course, costs for a particular project may vary widely from these typical costs. For example, all cost curves in Figures 2.1 and 2.2 were computed under an assumption of no respondent recruiting or compensation fees, although these may be a normal cost in many evaluation projects. Some of the cost items may already be available in-house to the evaluator, and so will not appear as direct costs for particular projects. Nonetheless, the relative costs of each method represented by the curves are generally valid.

Internet data collection is consistently cheaper than other forms of data collection. Just as face-to-face focus groups and one-on-one interviews are much more expensive per respondent than are mail or telephone question-

Figure 2.1. Completed Questionnaire Costs

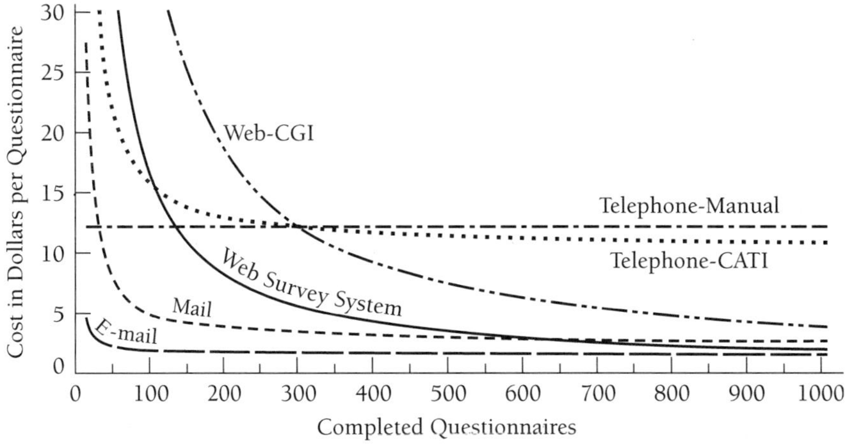

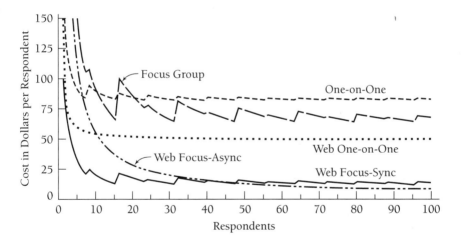

Figure 2.2. Interviewing Cost by Respondent

naires, Web focus groups and interviews are much more expensive per respondent to conduct than Web questionnaire research. But Web interviews and groups are clearly cheaper than face-to-face interviewing and focused discussion groups.

Populations and Representative Samples

Although the cost of Internet data collection makes it very attractive, there remains the problematic issue of the representativeness of the data obtained from on-line research. A representative sample has exactly the same characteristics, in the same proportions, as the full population. The term *random sample* is sometimes confused with *representative sample,* because a random selection of units from the population usually results (with some sampling error) in a representative sample. However, random choice of sample units is not the sole way of obtaining a representative sample. For example, if the population values of all variables that might bias the results are known, a representative sample can be obtained by quota sampling; that is, selecting sample units in exactly the same proportion that they exist in the population. In this case, a nonrandom procedure results in a representative sample. Unbiased random samples of any but very specialized populations are nearly impossible to obtain on the Internet. However, it is quite possible to obtain representative Internet samples of some (but not all) populations.

Populations for Internet Research

A convenient method of classifying populations is by the major rule for a unit's inclusion in the population. The utility of Internet evaluation research varies for differing types of populations.

Geographically Defined Population. Inclusion in this population is determined by geographical or political boundaries. An example of a geographically defined population is "all U.S. citizens." At present, a geographically defined population is often a poor fit for Internet data collection. For example, males are more likely to be Internet users than females, and middle-aged people use the Internet proportionally more than either older or younger persons. But recent research shows that the Internet user population is beginning to look much more like the whole population (Georgia Tech GVU Center, 1998), so with passing time the Internet may give more representative samples of the general geographically defined population.

Access to the Internet is a serious limitation in reaching a geographically defined population. Fewer than a quarter of the U.S. households regularly use Internet services (Lockhart and Detwiler, 1998), although over half of the U.S. population now has at least minimal access to the Internet, and use is increasing very rapidly. The Strategis Group (1999), a telecommunications research organization, reports that at the end of 1998 approximately 37 million U.S. adults were using the Internet daily at home, compared with 19 million in mid–1997. However, the worldwide percentage of use is much lower, and international Internet samples from a geographically defined population are very severely biased.

For the present, in geographically defined populations, Internet data collection is better seen as supplement to traditional methods of collecting data, rather than as a replacement for them. The portion of the target population that uses the Internet can be reached cheaply and quickly, while those not connected can be reached by mail, telephone, or in person. Supplementing traditional methods with Internet methods provides some immediate cost savings, and may provide better access to some segments of the population.

Demographically Defined Population. A demographically defined population is one whose primary inclusion rule is based on personal, political, or organizational characteristics. For example, a demographically defined population might be "middle management in high tech firms." The suitability of Internet research for these populations depends on Internet access and use by the desired demographic group.

Research participants can be screened on demographic responses to provide a sample that approximates the research population's demographic characteristics. Even if the basic population of Internet users does not match the demographically defined population, a sample that does match the desired population can be selected or screened from the overall population. The result is a nonrandom sample that may be representative of the population.

There is some controversy surrounding this screened-panel procedure, however (Bruzzone, 1999). Critics argue that whereas the resulting samples may be representative on simple demographics such as age and gender, they are biased in other, unmeasured, ways. For example, middle-aged male Internet users with average income may differ from similar middle-aged, average income males who do not use the Internet in many other ways. The nonusers may be less likely to be information seekers, may be less likely to work in information industries, and may differ in other important ways that might bias the results.

Service User Defined Population. Perhaps the best-suited population for Internet research is users of Internet information or commerce services. This category includes Web surfers at informational or educational sites, customers at e-commerce sites, and businesses that use Internet in day-to-day operations.

By definition, this population has 100 percent connectivity and members are often high users of Internet services. Users in commercial or nonprofit organizations are likely to have experience with the Internet and to recognize its convenience in replying to questionnaires. Home users of Internet services are also an excellent population to reach with Internet surveys, although their use frequency and speed of Internet connections are usually lower. For evaluation of services that are delivered by Internet (for example, Web information sites), Web-delivered evaluation questionnaires can be made part of the site's interaction with users with attendant high levels of motivation and participation from the respondents.

Individuals in service user defined populations can be reached via Internet in evaluation studies that do not necessarily involve services or programs that reside on the Internet, but whose users fall within the service user population. In this case, research participants would be recruited with traditional methods, and the respondent directed to the Internet interviewing site. Here, by capitalizing on the connectivity of service user populations, the Internet is used as a lower-cost replacement for traditional methods of interviewing respondents.

Cooperation Rates

Although access to Internet is one issue to consider when determining whether the data collection will result in a representative sample, the evaluator must also consider who is likely to take the time to participate in the evaluation, and who is not. If only a certain type of person participates in the evaluation, the sample will be biased and unrepresentative of the population.

Definitions of Cooperation Rate. The basic definition of the cooperation, response, or completion rate is the ratio of the number of sampled units who complete the research protocol to the number of units in the original sample (Fowler, 1984, p. 46). The extent to which this ratio decreases from 1.0 represents the potential for bias in the actual sample data. Note that a low cooperation rate does not automatically indicate an unrepresentative sample. It simply indicates that the sample might be biased.

In practice, this ratio is sometimes difficult to compute accurately. The original sample often contains units that are not actually part of the population. These must be eliminated. But the status of some of these sample units is ambiguous, and eliminating them may inflate the cooperation rate.

Consider the example in Table 2.2. In this hypothetical study, a banner link on a website requests that all visitors click on it to fill out a questionnaire evaluating the utility of the information on the site. Depending on how the researcher defines the basic sample size (the basis for the rate), the cooperation rate ranges from 20 to 67 percent for fully completed questionnaires. If the researcher uses the most conservative basis, the ratio of those who complete the entire questionnaire to the whole population of visitors to the site, the full cooperation rate is 20 percent. If the definition of cooperation is loosened to those who provide at least half of the information requested, the cooperation rate increases to 30 percent. If the basis is changed to those who provided at least one response, the partial cooperation rate is 75 percent and the full cooperation rate is 50 percent.

Cooperation rates reported for both traditional and Internet data collection suffer from lack of comparability because of the differing definitions of cooperation rate. Some less scrupulous commercial and academic researchers use very liberal definitions to produce attractive cooperation rates. However, these inflated rates mask the potential for sample bias.

Factors that Affect Cooperation Rates. Mail surveys typically report cooperation rates in the 15 to 30 percent range. This low cooperation rate requires careful interpretation of results by the evaluator, with particular attention given to possible sample biases. Telephone interviewing response rates are usually higher, in the 50 to 80 percent range. However, commer-

Table 2.2. Cooperation Rate Computations

	N	Base for Cooperation Computation			
		Visitors	Hits	Minimum Information	Half Information
Total visitors	10,000	1.00			
Hits on banner	5000	.50	1.0		
Provided at least one answer	4000	.40	.80	1.0	
Completed half or more	3000	.30	.60	.75	1.0
Completed full questionnaire	2000	.20	.40	.50	.67

cial research suppliers report that telephone cooperation rates have been falling over the past ten years.

Information about Internet cooperation rates is somewhat difficult to obtain. There exist far fewer Internet research projects from which to generalize than traditional data collection examples, and much of the existing Internet-based research is commercial and proprietary.

Nonetheless, reported cooperation rates for Web survey research seem to be very similar to those obtained for telephone interviewing. For example, Eveland and Dunwoody (1997) report a rate of 63 percent for a web-based survey evaluating the use of an NSF science information website. This is a great improvement over what might have been obtained with a mail questionnaire. Table 2.3 illustrates cooperation rates for a number of commercial studies (taken from Watt, 1999), and will serve as the basis for discussing some of the factors that affect cooperation rate.

Respondent Interest-Involvement in Evaluation Topic. Topics that are salient to respondents produce more cooperation. As shown in Table 2.3, an employee survey for a computer manufacturer had a full-questionnaire cooperation rate of 75 percent, while a questionnaire of comparable length that used a similar method of recruiting respondents had a much lower cooperation rate (56 percent). General site visitors to an on-line book retailer had a cooperation rate that was lower yet (45 percent). The employee survey involved issues of immediate salience to the respondents, and included the expectation that the results of the survey might have some impact on their jobs. The book retailer's questionnaire had no comparable level of importance to visitors to the e-commerce site.

Although setting the basic salience of the evaluation to the respondent is out of the evaluator's reach, some benefit can be obtained by communicating to the respondent the importance of the study and of cooperation (Watt and van den Berg, 1995, p. 363). In Web questionnaires, this can be accomplished with a strong opening page that explains the purpose of the study and the benefits of the results to the respondent or to a worthy cause. The Web's ability to deliver extensive text and audio-visual material in hypertext form may aid in establishing this salience to skeptical respondents.

Table 2.3. Cooperation Rates from Web Surveys

Client	Population	Recruitment Type	Incentive Type	Total Entries	Quick Exits	Completions Partial	Full	Percentage of Total	Percentage Including Partial
Investment broker	Individual investors	Web banner	$450 sweepstakes	4256	514	1076	2666	62.6	87.9
Peripherals manufacturer	Business users	Phone/quota	$5.00 for completion	299	11	59	229	76.6	96.3
Software manufacturer	Small hi-tech companies	Snailmail recruit	$1.00 token payment	57	2	17	38	66.7	96.5
High-tech marketing research	IT managers	Snailmail recruit	$1.00 token payment	357	11	65	281	78.7	96.9
Automobile manufacturer	General site visitors	Banner	Sweepstakes: bike	44641	14089	8905	21647	48.5	68.4
Computer manufacturer	Internal employees	Email recruit	None	932	36	202	694	74.5	96.1
Software designer	Trial download users	Email recruit	The software itself	1175	92	407	676	57.5	92.2
Financial market research	Mutual funds brokers	Banner	None	320	63	74	183	57.2	80.3
On-line book retailer-UK	General site visitors	Banner	Sweepstakes: bike	1500	591	240	669	44.6	60.6
On-line book retailer-Germany	General site visitors	Banner	Sweepstakes: bike	3316	1263	1020	1033	31.2	61.9

Incentives. If every respondent could be paid $1 million, there would be little problem in achieving 100 percent cooperation rates. With the realities of evaluation budgets, however, the size of incentives for participation in data collection must be balanced with the expected improvement in cooperation rate.

Incentives can serve as a substitute for salience of the evaluation topic. If the sample respondents are not likely to view the evaluation itself as personally important, they might be induced to cooperate by rewarding them for the time they spend in providing relevant information. However, providing inducements may introduce a negative side effect in some unmotivated respondents by persuading them to cooperate just enough to qualify for the incentive, without motivating them to give thought to their responses. The evaluator should build *consistency-check* questions into questionnaires to detect careless or malicious responses, and should have procedures to detect a similar lack of commitment to the task by focus group members.

The impact of the incentives on cooperation rate seems to be a function of three factors: the size of the incentive, the certainty of receiving it, and the time at which it is received. The relationship among these factors is not simple. For example, for relatively small incentives, larger is not necessarily better. Small token incentives have been shown to be as good as, or even better than, somewhat larger incentives (Mizes, Fleece, and Roos, 1984). Several entries in Table 2.3 illustrate the insensitivity of cooperation rate to incentives in the under-$10 range. In one case, a $1 incentive produced better cooperation than a $5 incentive.

As incentive size increases beyond the token level, however, cooperation rates tend to be positively related to the size of the incentive. In some business-to-business focus group research involving professionals as group members, it is not uncommon to provide each group member with a $100 incentive for participation. This is normally treated as compensation for the respondent's time, which includes travel time to and from a focus group facility. Use of the Internet for focus group interviewing may reduce the size of the incentive needed to gain the cooperation of these hard-to-get group participants, as the elimination of travel time reduces the time commitment required to cooperate.

There is growing evidence from on-line research firms that the possibility of receiving a large reward, in the form of a sweepstakes prize, for example, is more likely to increase cooperation rates than is the certainty of receiving a small incentive. Some controlled research evidence supports this conclusion (Kimelfeld, 1999). In Internet surveys with large numbers of respondents, the sweepstakes method of providing an incentive is the only practical procedure. The cost of preparing and mailing almost 22,000 incentive checks in the auto manufacturer's study summarized in Table 2.3 would have doubled the cost of the research project, regardless of the amount of the check. Instead, the survey respondent was entered in a sweepstakes for a single $500 bicycle, and the survey achieved a fairly good 49 percent cooperation rate with an unmotivated general sample.

There is some evidence in recruited samples that incentives received *before* participation in the research project are actually more effective than making the incentive contingent on completing the research protocol (McClanahan, 1998). This phenomenon has been known for some time to direct mail solicitors of contributions. Some charitable organizations include token gifts, such as preprinted address labels or loose stamps for return mail, with their solicitation. Apparently the act of receiving something of value or usefulness, even if it is very small, generates a kind of social contract that motivates recipients to comply with the request for their time or money. In the survey of IT managers summarized in Table 2.3, respondents were initially recruited by sending a mailed request with the promise of a $1 token payment upon completion of the Web survey. The cooperation rate with this recruitment was under 35 percent. The recruitment procedure was redesigned to include a $1 bill with the recruitment letter, and the project achieved a final 79 percent cooperation rate.

Recruitment. As illustrated above, the recruitment procedure can be critical to achieving high cooperation rates, and therefore representative samples. Passive recruitment from a website banner is, in general, less effective at producing cooperation than is contact via another medium. Depending upon the population, telephone, surface mail, or e-mail may be effective in recruiting sample members. Schaefer and Dillman (1998) report that methodologies for improving cooperation rates that have been developed for standard mail questionnaires will also work for e-mail questionnaires. Telephone provides the most personal connection. Surface mail can be used to send materials that increase the project's salience or for token incentives. The recruitment procedure typically includes directions to the on-line research site, and may include passwords that deny entry to the research location to anyone other than those recruited. Recruitment in several different media, coupled with restricted entry to the Internet research site, can be used to ensure a more representative sample.

E-mail can be used to recruit participants from populations with high Internet usage and to directly link them with a single mouse click to the survey or discussion site. This ease-of-use increases cooperation by making it possible for the respondent to complete the research immediately, without the effort of locating the address of the research site and linking to it at a later date.

Technological Factors. In Internet research, the software and hardware environment of the sample members is often critical in determining the cooperation rate. If the respondent must install software before being able to participate, cooperation rates will decrease. The exception to this is highly involved sample members, whose interest in the inquiry may motivate them to go to the trouble of downloading and installing client software.

In general, however, inquiry projects that use simple e-mail or standard Web browsers are more likely to have high cooperation, and Internet evaluation studies should always be designed to use the simplest and most widely distributed technology that will do the job.

Delay in response from the Web survey server or the chat host system will reduce the completion rate. Delays may be introduced by Internet congestion, server systems that are undersized, or by inadequate client software. The impact of network congestion can be seen in the last two entries in Table 2.3. In these projects, identical surveys were hosted in the United States but presented to respondents in the United Kingdom and Germany. Network latencies to the United Kingdom were fairly low, although still somewhat higher than typical U.S. response times. The U.K. survey achieved a 45 percent cooperation rate with uninvolved site visitors. The German survey had much higher network latencies because of congested net links, and the full cooperation rate was only 31 percent. Many respondents abandoned the survey because of the annoyance with delays in the responses of the Web server.

The prescriptions to the evaluator are fairly clear. Synchronous on-line research should be scheduled, when possible, for times when the Internet traffic is lower: evenings, early mornings, and lunch hours. Asynchronous research should be placed on a server with sufficient capacity to handle the peak usage. This peak is very pronounced with Web surveys. It is common for half the responses to a survey to be completed within forty-eight hours.

To illustrate the "bursty" nature of Web survey responses, suppose 10,000 potential respondents are recruited by e-mail, with a linked Web survey, and the basic cooperation rate is 50 percent. Five thousand respondents will eventually fill out the survey, but 2,500 will try to do so in the first two days. However, the time at which these 2,500 will respond will not be distributed evenly across two days. There will be sharp peaks immediately after the e-mail recruitment message is received, and at times the respondents normally read their e-mail: early mornings and right after lunch for business or organizational users, and early evening for home users.

The host Web survey system must be able to handle these bursts of activity without introducing significant delays in response. In the example above, it is likely that several times during the two-day period, 100 persons will be simultaneously using the Web server. The hardware running the server and the Web survey software must be sized to meet this peak demand, and the bandwidth of the server's Internet connection must be sufficient.

The peak demand can be spread over a longer time period by sending out the e-mail recruitments at intervals, rather than as a single-batch mailing. This adds some extra effort, but will pay off in higher completion rates, as the peak demand at any single time will be reduced, thus minimizing the server delay in responding.

Strategies for On-Line Data Collection

The primary requirement for conducting on-line data collection is that the population to be reached is compatible with the group of Internet users available. The most appropriate populations are those defined by Internet use itself, or those located in organizations that have high levels of connectivity. Failure to match the Internet population to the target population can result in unrepresentative samples.

There have recently been some indications that the special nature of the Internet user population may be less important in some areas than originally thought. Bruzzone (1999) reports on six projects that compared traditional data collection (mainly telephone interviewing) with Internet data collection. This study, sponsored by the Advertising Research Foundation, found some significant differences between the demographics of the Internet research respondents and respondents who participated in the traditional marketing research studies. However, traditional and Web survey studies produced the same results, even though the research populations differed on demographic variables. The same conclusion was reached by a packaged goods manufacturer who compared Web surveys with mall consumer research. Although it is somewhat risky to project consumer research findings to other social or evaluation research projects, there remains the possibility that on-line research may provide valid results even when the targeted research populations do not completely match the Internet user population.

The second strategic decision involves the kind of communication setting that Internet research provides as compared to that provided by traditional data collection methods. For questionnaire administration, there is little to lose with Internet methods, and much to gain. The act of filling out the questionnaire by a respondent differs little whether on paper or on screen. However, Web questionnaires can offer flexible administration protocols, pleasing aesthetics, and convenience of submission that can make them superior to paper versions. Web questionnaires can be supplemented with animated graphical and audio-visual material that enables them to present respondents with material that would be impossible with any traditional survey technique.

The benefits of synchronous interviews and focus groups are more problematic. Web discussions, with their limited bandwidths, offer different communication environments than face-to-face or even telephone interviewing. On-line focus groups have different dynamics and patterns of interaction than do face-to-face groups because of the limitations of the technology. The challenge for the evaluator is to determine whether the mediating technology chosen for the project distorts the results, is neutral, or whether it may even enhance them.

This leads to the next consideration: matching the inquiry topic to the data collection technique. In a synchronous group discussion of sensitive or embarrassing topics, for example, the partial anonymity provided by on-line interaction may actually improve the outcome. But trying to conduct a free-form group discussion that requires rapid interaction and immediate feedback with an asynchronous text conference may produce poor results.

The complexity of the project will affect the choice of technique. E-mail questionnaires may be quite acceptable for a simple questionnaire with a few questions, whereas a full Web survey or CGI questionnaire may be needed for complex questionnaires with many logical branches. For extensive projects, full collaborative tools with audio-visual connections may be needed.

The type and complexity of the software needed to participate in the data collection is also a major strategic decision. As with other decisions, this is often a trade-off: richer data can be collected with more complex software (for example, audio-visual interaction), but the demands of more powerful computer systems to run the software, more computer knowledge by respondents who must install and use the software, and the requirement of higher bandwidth connections for many programs, may limit the possible respondents and bias the sample. The rule of thumb is simplicity, but that must be balanced against the need for advanced data collection features.

Prospects for Future On-Line Research

The Internet will be used increasingly as a location or method for all social research, including evaluation studies. There are a number of factors that inspire confidence in this prediction.

First, more services that require evaluation are likely to have a presence on the Internet. This places their users in the most desirable population for on-line research: users who are immediately accessible.

Second, the lower-cost, higher-speed nature of Internet data collection will benefit projects evaluating goods or services that are not Internet related but whose users are on-line. Lower-cost data collection means larger samples, more statistical power, and more useful results. The collection of data in a form that can be immediately analyzed cuts the time required for a project and thus increases its timeliness.

As discussed above, selecting more representative samples from demographically or geographically defined populations in the future will depend upon the overall Internet user population becoming more like the general population. According to a series of over-time surveys done by the Georgia Tech GVU Center (1998), the rapid increase in home connection to the Internet is moving the demographics of the U.S. Internet user population to more resemble the U.S. census figures each year. This makes the Internet a more suitable location for research on demographically defined populations each succeeding year. In addition, the rapid growth of home use in the general population (Strategis Group, 1999) makes reaching many research populations with Internet research tools much more viable.

The wider distribution and use of standard Internet communication tools such as e-mail and Web browsers, and the growing standardization of communication software protocols for applications such as synchronous videoconferencing, will make it much easier to reach research populations with advanced procedures in the near future. The widespread adoption of Java-language in Web browsers and other user applications will permit researchers to move sophisticated computer-based research tools that feature real-time interaction with respondents from their current laboratory settings to the Internet.

A third event that will increase the importance of the Internet for evaluation is the prospect of much higher bandwidth to homes, businesses, and organizations. Internet2, now being tested and developed by university-business consortiums, will increase the central backbone speeds by a factor of 100. Services such as DSL (digital subscriber line) offered by telephone companies or cable modem access from cable communications companies promise to increase Internet speed to homes by a factor of 20 to 200. These speed increases will make data collection techniques involving audio-visual communication, such as synchronous Web focus groups, much easier to carry out, as audio-visual conferencing software becomes as common as Web browsers are today.

The combination of low-cost data collection with advanced software tools means that Internet-based evaluation will probably move from reaching restricted populations and supplementing traditional forms of data collection to becoming a predominant location for evaluation inquiry.

References

Baym, N. K. "The Emergence of Community in Computer-Mediated Communication." In S. G. Jones (ed.), *Cybersociety: Computer-Mediated Communication and Community.* Thousand Oaks, Calif.: Sage, 1995, pp. 138–163.

Bertot, J. C., and McClure, C. R.. "Electronic Surveys: Methodological Implications for Using the World Wide Web to Collect Survey Data." *Proceedings of the ASIS Annual Meeting.* Silver Spring, Md.: American Society for Information Science, 1996, 33, pp. 173–85.

Bruzzone, D. "The Top 10 Insights About the Validity of Conducting Research Online." Advertising Research Foundation, [http://www.arf.amic.com/Webpages/onlineresearch99/LA_99_top10.htm]. 1999.

Dillman, D. A.. "The Design and Administration of Mail Surveys." *Annual Review of Sociology,* 1991, 17, 225–49.

Eveland, W. P., and Dunwoody, S. "Users and Navigation Patterns of a Science World Wide Web Site for the Public." Paper presented at the international conference on the Public Understanding of Science and Technology, Chicago, Ill., 1997.

Fowler, F. J.. *Survey Research Methods.* Beverly Hills, Calif: Sage, 1984.

Fulop, M. P. "Using the World Wide Web to Conduct a Needs Assessment." *Performance Improvement,* 1997, 36 (6), 22–27.

Georgia Tech Graphics, Visualization, and Usability Center. User Surveys. [http://www.gvu.gatech.edu/user_surveys/]. 1998.

Kimelfeld, Y. "Transactional Advertising on the Web and in Print Promotions: A Cross-Media Comparison." Paper presented to the International Communication Association, San Francisco, 1999.

Lockhart, D. C., and Detwiler, R. J. "Internet Surveys: A Description of the Demographics." *Quirk's Marketing Research Review*, 1998, *12* (7), 40–46.

McClanahan, P., vice president, Boston Research Group. Personal communication, 1998.

Mizes, J. S., Fleece, E. L., and Roos, C. "Incentive for Increasing Return Rates: Magnitude Levels, Response Bias, and Format." *Public Opinion Quarterly*, 1984, *48*, 794–800.

Persichitte, K. A. "Conducting Research on the Internet: Strategies for Electronic Interviewing." Proceedings of the national convention of the Association for Educational Communications and Technology, Albuquerque, N.M., 1997. (ERIC ED409860).

Schaefer, D. R., and Dillman, D. A. "Development of a Standard E-mail Methodology: Results of an Experiment." *Public Opinion Quarterly*, 1998, *62* (3), 378–97.

Strategis Group "Internet Use Becoming a Daily Essential." [http://www.strategis-group.com/press/pubs/interuse.html]. 1999.

Watt, J., and van den Berg, S. *Research Methods for Communication Science*. Boston: Allyn and Bacon, 1995.

Watt, J. "Using the Internet for Quantitative Survey Research." *Quirk's Marketing Research Journal*, 1997, *11* (6), 18–19.

Watt, J. H. "Internet-Based Surveys." *Upgrade: Journal of the Software and Information Industry Association*, 1999, *16* (1), 10–15.

JAMES H. WATT is professor of communication sciences at the University of Connecticut. His research centers on new communication technology, computer-mediated communication, and marketing communication. He is currently developing Web-based survey research systems and investigating elements of effective Web advertising.

3

The authors focus on using technological support to observe user behaviors and gather feedback in the evaluation of software and virtual environments such as websites.

Evaluating On-Line Environments: Tools for Observing Users and Gathering Feedback

Robert H. Rieger, Amanda Sturgill

Evaluating on-line media products such as computer programs and websites offers the promise that the technology that enables the media can also enable novel methods of evaluation. But assessing Internet media such as websites, chat spaces, and electronic mail networks can be difficult owing to the challenges of gathering, organizing, and sharing useful data. For example, the audience can remain relatively anonymous, tried-and-true techniques do not always translate to electronic environments, and, because data are so easily generated, the amount of information collected can be overwhelming. Media- and technology-rich environments need equally rich data collection and analysis tools that can capture the system's complexity and provide useful representations of human-computer interactions. In this chapter, we consider the use of technology to evaluate technology, with an emphasis on recording user interactions with systems and gathering user feedback within the context of a multimedia environment.

Although this chapter focuses on analyzing electronic and networked environments—such as a virtual Web community, an on-line literature database, or a records management system—the concepts and strategies discussed here can be made relevant in other evaluation efforts. For example, researchers can reconsider unobtrusive data collection techniques in all types of programs in light of new offerings for assessing technologically based ones. Can unobtrusive measures be used to collect agency statistics or productivity measurements in novel ways? The old turn-stile attendance counting system used in public agencies, for example, can take on new significance when applied in an integrated and synchronized manner, such as by making counts visually informative, continuously available, and integrated into other feedback systems. If data are available to program reviewers and organizers on an up-to-the-minute basis, the relevance and usefulness of data are strengthened. We have seen, for example, libraries borrow techniques from technology assessors to provide key audiences with consistent and timely data on usage statistics, patron requests, and reference services. In health care and court settings, new prototypes in visualization (Plaisant and others, 1999) demonstrate how complex patient histories or court data, collected without the use of computers, can take on new meaning when presented graphically using time lines, color, and other multimedia. The field of data mining—the use of computerized analysis tools to look for patterns and relationships in data—is another example. Even if the data do not relate to computer-based programs or tools, the technology of data mining can still prove fruitful in examining it.

Because many of the methods presented in this chapter do raise significant ethical concerns in light of their abilities to monitor behaviors in covert ways, it is especially important for researchers and evaluators who use these methods to address informed consent, privacy, confidentiality, and other human subject issues. For example, when using electronic mail to collect information, the evaluator has no way to confirm the age of the respondent and no way to ensure the privacy of information that may be presented. Disturbingly, most human subjects contracts are not prepared to respond to the relatively new informed consent concerns generated by technological advances. The leader of human subjects offices, the National Institutes of Health, has offered advice on a case-by-case basis as technological methods of data collection have challenged the opportunities for privacy and age control available to researchers. Given the critical importance of these issues, editors Gay and Bennington have focused the concluding chapter of this volume on the ethical concerns surrounding this type of investigation.

The information presented here is based on our participation as evaluators on a number of library and museum technology initiatives, including the Making of America I and II, Museum Education Site License Project, Global Digital Museum, and Art Museum Image Consortium (AMICO) University Testbed. We begin the chapter by exploring relevant literature and defining key issues and terms, then describe several tools and techniques for collecting data and user reactions within on-line environments such as the initiatives we have evaluated. A final section supports our position that synchronous and integrated evaluations that make full use of newly emerging tools are a promising direction for evaluators responsible for documenting and assessing the quality of electronic environments.

New Environments, New Issues

Evaluators must consider in context the new technological systems appearing all around us, such as websites for information dissemination, electronic payment distribution systems for social services, and caseload databases with networked access. We suggest that evaluators develop a functional understanding of how the technology is used within a particular context. Current approaches to the evaluation of electronic systems have broadened to include multifaceted methods of data collection and analysis (Marchionini and Plaisant, 1996). Such an approach requires considering the interactions among the various groups that are working to define and develop digital environments. We encourage a framework for evaluation based on a social construction of technology (SCOT) model, which considers the multiple social perspectives surrounding the development of new technologies (Kilker and Gay, 1998). The SCOT model encourages evaluators to consider the interactions and complexities among the various groups that are working to define and develop digital environments. Simple measurements of technological performance (for example, the number of "hits" to a home page) are inadequate when isolated from data about the social structure within which the systems are designed or for which they are planned. SCOT encourages a group-centered approach to all evaluation data collection, analysis reporting, and usage.

For all evaluations of technology (similar to evaluations of face-to-face programs), technology evaluators can rely on different kinds of data from a variety of sources, such as usage statistics, interviews with computer systems experts, and user focus groups. The claims that can be made based on this multimethod approach can be richer, better-substantiated, and more useful to readers (Greene and McClintock, 1985). A goal is to produce a "thick description" of the environment, referring, for example, to a detailed representation of the information-seeking process of users (Geertz, 1973).

There seems to be much promise in the use of technology to evaluate technology. Researchers and evaluators have for many years relied upon computers in evaluations of multimedia environments. Early computer tracking systems allowed inquirers to record system usage, alert developers to problem areas, and save records of interactions for later use. Today's approaches have similar functions, plus the ability to intersect multimedia, network, and participatory environments. They not only allow evaluators to gather data from the electronic systems as they are being used, but also simplify and improve the integration of other data such as observations, interviews, documents produced, and video and audio records. The technologies support evaluators as they analyze the data and develop their interpretations. When combined, these data paint a rich and textured description of users, the multimedia, and the interactions that offers a holistic picture of the state of the artifact or program being evaluated.

Revisiting Traditional Evaluation Issues

In this section we consider how common issues familiar to evaluators change when located in electronic environments. To what extent, for example, do popular evaluation approaches—needs assessment, program planning, formative evaluation, and summative evaluation—map onto the testing and evaluation of electronic systems? Table 3.1 presents a list of evaluation issues and the range of choices offered.

Types of Measurement. The two basic measurements that have been used in human-computer interaction evaluations are (1) observing user behavior with the system, and (2) collecting user opinions about the system. User behaviors can be tracked via computer, recorded with videotape or screen recorders, or charted by a human observer. They can also be self-reported by the users via a standardized instrument. User opinions can be gathered by means of a prepared survey (administered by computer or on paper), focus groups, or individual interviews, or possibly inferred from user behavior observations. One hybrid setup involves audio or videotaping testers as they provide a verbal description of both their actions and opinions. This is akin to talk-aloud protocols used by evaluators. The chapter by Mathison, Meyer, and Vargas in this volume addresses this protocol in detail.

Evaluation Audiences. Audiences can be generalized as (1) expert developers, or (2) end users. Expert developers are individuals from both the technical fields (such as programmers, webmasters, network administrators, and hardware experts) and the content development groups (such as psychologists, social workers, program administrators, librarians, funding representatives, and agency staff). End users can be both members of the actual audience (users) for whom the system is designed and "surrogates" who are demographically similar and share common motivations with end users. Surrogates are often more conveniently available than end users. In one website evaluation project, as the site was developed, opinions were sought from staff, visitors, and programmers who worked on museum websites. In this case, each of these audiences brought a different expertise to bear on the development of the site. Staff were experts in the presentation of museum information, programmers were experts in technical possibilities, and visitors or end users were experts in what would make this site valuable to the site's intended audience.

Presence of Evaluators. Similar to traditional evaluations, an obtrusive presence implies that the system evaluator is directly noticed and acknowledged by the test user, such as when they sit beside each other during a talk-aloud test or conduct overt testing either in-person or through a chat or bulletin board style discussion. An unobtrusive presence implies the

Table 3.1. Issues and Choices in Electronic Evaluation

Issues	Choices		
Types of measurement	Observing user interactions	↔	Collecting user opinions
Audiences	Expert developers	↔	End users
Presence of evaluators	Obtrusive	↔	Unobtrusive
Timing of data collection	Synchronous	↔	Asynchronous
Timing of analysis and reporting	Synchronous	↔	Asynchronous

opposite, that testers do not regularly notice an evaluator presence. Many of the data collection tools presented in this chapter, such as user tracking systems, offer the advantage of unobtrusive presence. Obtrusive methods can also offer distinct advantages. In one evaluation of software, a technique called monitoring was used in which an evaluator sat with the end user recording interactions over time on a spread sheet. In addition to recording interactions that the users were expected to make, having a human evaluator present meant that unexpected reactions to the software could be recorded. These unexpected reactions became some of the more interesting results of the evaluation. When evaluating systems over a period of time with obtrusive methods, investigators expect obtrusiveness to diminish over time. This is similar to leaving a video camera in someone's home. After a while, the participants grow accustomed to the camera as part of the environment and it becomes less distracting.

Timing of Data Collection. Information and feedback can be collected during the testing of the system (*synchronous*) and before or after system usage (*asynchronous*). Compared with noncomputer evaluations, evaluators of electronic systems can make greater use of data collection timing options. Although interrupting users and asking for feedback can be difficult in evaluating traditional media and programs, simple electronic prompts buried in electronic presentations can minimize the impact of interruptions. Synchronous data collection has the advantage of immediacy, whereas asynchronous offers more time for review and reflection. Synchronous collection may also allow the user to collect data in the context of that which is being evaluated. One feedback tool allows the user to click on an evaluation icon in a website and answer a question about a particular aspect of the site that appears in a pop-up window.

Analysis Timing of Data and Reporting. Traditional methods of data analysis and reporting are mostly asynchronous because they take place after or outside the activity being evaluated. New and emerging technologies have allowed data analysis and reporting to take place in a more dynamic and synchronous fashion. Data from Web-based surveys and other collection methods can be immediately and automatically analyzed after each new record is added to create a more active reporting system. Inquirers can conveniently review data in an up-to-the-minute fashion and from a time-series perspective. The results of analysis can also be fed back to the end user, as in the case of an instant poll that shows up on a website. The overall benefit is that iterative development cycles are shortened, allowing developers to stay more precisely directed on their goal. In an evaluation of a website presenting museum collections, there were several efforts to collect data from experts and end users. The data that resulted were analyzed and the results were available to the evaluators immediately. This allowed the development of a sort of community of evaluators who were able to build on ideas put forth from other users. In this way, the evaluation by electronic means captured some of the best aspects of face-to-face focus groups.

Recording User Interactions

One of the great advantages to computers is that the system leaves abundant documentation and performance evidence. This section explores the goals and strategies for using tracking tools and other unobtrusive measures to assess computer environments. *User tracking* refers to monitoring a user or groups of users to document how they function in an electronic environment. Investigators can choose to run integrated or companion systems in the background of a program that record the many interactions. These systems can record meticulously the number of keystrokes, content items seen by the user, navigation strategies, and paths constructed through the program. These tracks require no effort on the part of the test user and minimal attention of the inquirer after the initial setup of the system. As previously noted, tracking data are most effectively used in tandem with other evaluation approaches. For example, a user's navigation pattern can be recreated into a visual "player piano" that can be used during an interview or focus group as a conversation stimulus. Or website usage statistics can be posted to a shared evaluation space, allowing research collaborators baseline data from which to expand or focus their investigation.

Although tracking systems allow a great deal of data to be collected relatively unobtrusively, these data can be difficult to deal with because of the volume of data generated. The evaluator will be tempted to take a reductionist approach in the use of the data, which may undermine the rich method of data collection. Dealing with vast data can also be extraordinarily time consuming.

Log File Analysis. All of today's popular Web servers generate log files containing vast data about user navigation that evaluators can access either directly through a text editor or through one of the many log file analysis packages commercially available. For example:

Surf Report [http://www.bienlogic.com/SurfReport/]
Web Manage (Net Intellect) [http://www.netintellect.com/netintellect30.html]
WWW Stat [http://www.ics.uci.edu/pub/Websoft/wwwstat/]
Logdoor [http://www2.opendoor.com/logdoor/]

Many server software packages also include some type of log analysis tool. Number and origin of site visitors, top requested pages or graphics files, server activity by time or date, and number of errors are among the many measurements available through the log file. By measuring the length of time between selected links, the amount of time spent on individual pages can be estimated. In our own lab, the log file is regularly analyzed to evaluate the effectiveness of the lab website in serving user needs. Another common analysis is top requested page by average time spent on each page.

What happens if evaluators are more interested in reviewing the usage patterns of individual users? Although the data are usually aggregated by log file analysis tools to see general trends, log files can record information, such as navigation patterns or page preferences, generated by a single computer. By using commercial analysis software, investigators can specify a computer's Internet Protocol (IP) address in order to zero in on a particular computer. In a lab test setting, this can then be translated to identify use by specific users. Another simple method for tracking individual users involves hiding "on-load" commands within an html (HyperText Markup Language) file so that each time an action takes place some type of report is generated to an external file. This is useful for websites that contain dynamic html or JavaScript applications that do not necessarily report to log or other record-keeping files. Similar to log files, investigators with access to user hardware can also view history (.hst) files or cache files to monitor website usage.

Screen Recorders. Investigators can record user sessions through a number of ways: by setting up a camera over the shoulder of a tester, positioning an audio recorder nearby, or using a computer-based recording device such as

ScreenCam [http://www.lotus.com/home.nsf/welcome/screencam]
SnagIt [http://www.snagit.com/]

Such recordings can be considered both an effort to track users and, if users are encouraged to comment as they move about the system, an approach at gathering user feedback. Video and audio records are time-consuming to review. Short clips, once isolated, can be powerful illustrations of user interactions. Web streaming technologies now allow for the sample clips to be delivered to evaluators alongside other data reports. Evaluators and the audience for the evaluation need to be cautious that short excerpts are not taken out of context. In an evaluation of a video- and text-based collaboration system, asking 30 people to participate generated 45 hours of videotape for coding and analysis. This is a rich data set, but one that is difficult to deal with both in terms of evaluator time in reviewing all of these tapes and in presenting such a mountain of data about rich interactions.

Persistent Cookies. Although they have alarmed many people concerned with Internet privacy issues, another option for gathering information from visitors to websites involves the use of persistent cookies. A cookie is information placed on a user's hard drive upon visiting a website. Cookies give Web servers the ability to identify unique users. With a cookie on your hard drive, for example, you may be able to eliminate extensive log-in requirements at each session. Advertisers and news agencies say cookies allow for customization, an important advantage for both servers and users. Unlike other methods for collecting data about users of network resources, cookies are attractive because the information persists from session to session, and allows the Web server to recognize a user as having visited from the same computer as before (Dern, 1997). Regardless of promise, in general cookies do offer the potential for abuse in terms of privacy, virus issues, and commercial interests.

That is not to say that they should be completely ignored by evaluators. More recent browsers offer safeguards by giving users much greater control over cookie distribution and allowing them to set their browsers to prompt them each time a cookie is about to be sent. Cookies offer the capacity for website administrators and evaluators to gather more information than that available from the log file. For example, if an agency wished to assist new users of an information database, cookies can help identify them without requiring users to overtly enter that information. Without disturbing users, evaluators could then examine how users enter information, how they search, what search terms and constructions they use, what resources they receive, and what they look at. In a single observation or multiple representations over time, inquirers can easily and efficiently track user behaviors within a system via cookies. If users become aware of the use of cookies (for example if their browser informs them), it may cause their behaviors to change and no longer be representative.

Agents. Another interesting method for collecting data in an unobtrusive way involves the use of agents. In an evaluation context, agents are software designed to use the Internet to collect information about application usage by "traveling" to remote sites and monitoring activity. They are especially well-designed for automatic data collection for large-scale, distributed systems. A typical evaluation agent scenario is described by Hilbert and Redmiles (1998).

1. Developers design application and create agents.
2. Agents are deployed to run on users' computers.
3. Agents observe users as they interact with the application.
4. Agents detect unexpected usage patterns (called *mismatches)* and collect data and user feedback.
5. Agents report back to developers to inform application evolution.
6. Developers refine the application, the agents, or both.

In its simplest sense, software can be prepared to monitor usage and report various behaviors back to the evaluators. Hilbert and Redmiles offer an "expectation-driven" approach to agent usage (1998). Developers have numerous expectations about how users will use such systems. When users perform tasks contrary to expectations, this can trigger a local agent to do one or both of the following: (1) send a report of the event to developers; (2) prompt a user to enter feedback based on that particular event. For example, if a user initiates his or her use of a website by choosing a complex first link, the agent could open a dialogue box on the user's computer seeking information about that particular action. In more advanced applications of agents, the software can provide information to the evaluators, and the evaluators can instruct the agent on the fitness of the information, allowing the agent to modify the information it gathers. Although research on this type of "learning agent" is fairly well established

[http://agents.www.media.mit.edu/groups/agents/_],

it has not been adopted in the evaluation context yet.

Explorations into the use of agents in evaluating new technologies are really just beginning. Like the use of cookies, more investigation is needed in issues of informed consent, human subjects concerns, and privacy and security of test users.

Automated Services. One final method to evaluate websites involves the use of commercial testing services that explore your site files and evaluate such elements as hyperlinks, html coding, image optimization, and server performance. The cost for these services can range from free to several thousand dollars. At time of publication, a sample of some of the free sites included

http://www.websitegarage.com/
http://www.netmechanic.com/
http://watson.addy.com/

The first two offer "upgrade" packages that, for a fee, will conduct more comprehensive analysis of the site and revisit the site on a regular basis to analyze and report findings. These services are completely automated; their computers retrieve the URL and instantly conduct an analysis and generate a report. No human actually looks at the site, thus limiting the kinds of feedback available.

User Artifacts. Other background measurements refer more directly to the successes and failures of users' interactions. Performance can be measured, for example, by the number of correct hits a user gets from a digital image collection website, or how efficiently a user recognizes the most logical path within a hyperlinked environment. User artifacts, such as postings to a networked bulletin board, can be analyzed over time to reveal trends. External scores and metrics can be applied in similar ways. In an evaluation of a course-support software system, students were able to post comments and questions to an electronic bulletin board. These comments and questions were printed and subjected to a traditional content analysis that allowed the evaluator to objectively see the patterns of interaction that developed—who talked to whom and what was said.

Contextual User Feedback

This section focuses on gathering feedback from users and expert developers of electronic systems. The "tried-and-true" methods of obtaining direct input have included survey questionnaires, personal interviews, and focus groups. Although these face-to-face and paper-and-pencil methods still have a place, the Internet now allows their migration to a networked environment. Using Java and dynamic html, evaluators can create unique response methods designed to present a more naturalistic test environment for users to view media. This approach allows feedback to occur in a situated context; the look and feel of the feedback medium is similar to the environment being analyzed, promoting less disruption for test users and, quite possibly, more valid and accurate responses. It also allows investigators to gather information easily from a distributed community of users and to promote dialogue among users and evaluators through a networked channel.

The tools and techniques offered below represent some practices that have been used for many years in interface evaluation and iterative design, and others that are newly emerging based on new programming languages, such as Java. If recent development cycles are any indication, specific tools developed in the near future may quickly overtake those presented here. However, the principle goal of grounding user feedback attempts within the system, thereby minimizing disruption, remains solid.

Windows and Frames. A relatively simple and effective method of eliciting extensive user feedback on Web environments involves programming a survey in a separate Web page, or a frame on the same Web page and adding links to the various sections. Testers can easily move back and forth between the main site and the questions. The links can provide users with instant access to various parts of the website. For example, if an inquirer wants testers to view a specific section, such a link could be incorporated into the survey page. Once the entire survey has been completed, either in a frame or a separate page, users can submit the data back to the evaluation server. Using this method is more useful if the users are interested in participating in the evaluation. This method will be used when we evaluate museum websites by querying museum programmers.

OnMouseOver and Timed Input. An "onmouseover" command in html allows inquirers to embed survey questions into a Web document with their appearance in a floating window triggered by one or a combination of mouse actions. If a user drags a cursor over a particular graphic element or other object, this can trigger the opening of a question box, allowing both numeric or open-ended responses. The trigger elements may or may not be visible to the user.

Another option is to have a similar question box appear on a timed basis or after data have been entered by the user. For example, after users have been on a page for a set amount of time, such as a minute, a dialogue box opens on their screen to request input. Again, user willingness to participate is critical in this method. The sudden appearance of floating windows can negatively bias an unwilling or unprepared user to the artifact being evaluated, thus allowing the evaluation method to seriously impact the evaluation process.

Web Page Annotators. There are Web annotation software packages, such as Hot Off the Web <http://www.hotofftheweb.com/>, which allow users to make comments directly on Web-like documents. Any Universal Resource Locator (URL) can be called up from inside the custom browser. The program then presents the page as a single snapshot; hyperlinks and other html or Javascript codes become inactive. Reviewers are then able to post comments and other annotations using small "post-it" style notes, stickers, highlight pens, and drawing tools. The marked-up page can then be saved as html with all annotations saved in the same folder. These pages can then be served for distributed review or viewed from the desktop. This also has the advantage of letting groups of users review and respond to each other's annotations, thus offering some of the benefits of focus group research. A primitive version of this is the annotation feature in Microsoft Word, which allows evaluators to embed colored annotations directly in a text document. The authors of this chapter live 1,500 miles apart and used this feature in the chapter's editing.

On-line Concept Mapping. Trochim (1999) describes concept mapping as "a structured process, focused on a topic or construct of interest, involving input from one or more participants, that produces an interpretable pictorial view (concept map) of their ideas and concepts and how these are interrelated." Group members can visually map their ideas about a particular topic. Trochim has been an innovator at moving traditional concept mapping evaluation techniques to a networked environment. For example, stakeholders can communicate their preferences of system functionality electronically via a website. Inquirers can then work in the same environment to organize the statements. Trochim's system then generates concept maps based on user input.

Talk-Aloud and Usage Monitoring Methods. Our research lab has frequently relied on a combined talk-aloud and usage monitoring protocol designed to elicit user reactions to computer systems. Testers and evaluators sit together with video and audio recording devices in place. Testers are encouraged to describe their actions and opinions as they navigate through a system. Depending on the goals, the evaluators can shepherd the user through the system by following a strict or loose scenario. As a general rule, the earlier in the iterative design process, the more active a role taken by the accompanying evaluator. Developers often need to "fill in the blanks" when systems are in early stages and many of the functions are only available as design prototypes. Upon completion, testers are usually asked to complete a questionnaire, either paper or electronic, designed to gather more overarching reflections and observations. The recordings are then transcribed and, if needed, highlight tapes are made by selecting and editing together noteworthy segments of the sessions. This method suffers from the limitations of obtrusive methods mentioned above. This technique was recently used in an evaluation of search engines. Users talked aloud about their methods in using the engines and their ruminations were recorded. Samples of the user feedback were made into a tape that became part of the evaluation deliverable. Obviously this type of reporting requires the evaluator to be punctilious about including representative bits of feedback.

Synchronous and Integrated Data Collection

The tools and techniques described above, in addition to making evaluation more situated and unobtrusive, tend to lean more toward evaluation methods that are "synchronous and integrated." As opposed to asynchronous user-feedback methods—which generally involve gathering reactions upon completion of a task or review and reporting in a formal process—synchronous approaches employ extensive use of networked technologies both to collect data and report findings in a dynamic and instantaneous fashion. This technique seems to offer several advantages over asynchronous methods, including a promise for better integration of the evaluation and software design process. The same tools used to distribute information itself can be used to improve the design of that information. Users are able to provide feedback as they use the system, thus allowing designers to make better use of evaluation data. Synchronous efforts attempt to place evaluation in the context of actual usage. Consider, for example, having website evaluation activities a click or two away, or even open alongside, a Web product. Although users can certainly complete a paper questionnaire next to a computer screen, the need to switch between modes may be annoying or diminish the user's sense of context. Another advantage is that synchronous evaluations can improve response rates because of convenience, respondent motivation, and a greater sense of relevance and context.

Additional issues regarding synchronous and asynchronous evaluations include

- Exposure: Asynchronous evaluations prescribe that data are to be collected based on a "one-shot" exposure to a static product. Synchronous evaluations rely on collecting data continuously in response to versions that are in a constant state of development.
- Iterative design cycle: Asynchronous evaluation makes an iterative design process logistically difficult. An on-line, or synchronous, approach encourages continuous improvement based on feedback. The iterative design cycle is shortened. Multimedia authors can receive suggestions, respond, and retest.
- Response rate: Synchronous evaluations can improve response rates because of convenience, respondent motivation, and a greater sense of relevance and context. Asynchronous evaluations can appear more inconsequential to test users, thus creating nonresponses, which can destroy the representativeness of the respondent group.
- Respondent bias: From a technological standpoint, asynchronous data collection, such as through follow-up surveys or interviews, offer a minimally challenging feedback method. Respondents are usually comfortable with these methods. Synchronous methods, however, require some level of comfort with technology. Results would seem to be skewed toward more technologically literate respondents, thereby increasing respondent bias.

However, this limitation may be ameliorated by the fact that most participants who would be test users would probably be sufficiently facile with the technology or similar technologies (for example, computers in general, if not a particular piece of software).

Use of synchronous, on-line evaluation tools offers a great deal of promise for better integrating the evaluation and design processes. Users and designers can participate in a "community of review" that provides for more frequent updating of projects and a greater number of voices to improve decision making. All collaborators in a project can work together to design and interpret user reactions. The feedback from different collaborators can be built into a knowledge base for all to draw from in improving the product. Finally, reports can be easily customized according to reader preferences.

This approach is not without its drawbacks, however. Creating on-line environments requires collaborators to either acquire or retain staff who have the necessary skills. Also, assuming that users can evaluate the product in the process of using it may be a naive proposition that should be tested in further research. Finally, the method obviously works only as long as users have on-line access. Again, such approaches need further testing and refinement. Future systems, for example, might want to examine the effect reflection has on respondents' views of the products, perhaps by including users with different levels of facility with technology and products like the one being tested.

Conclusion

Regardless of the goal of a particular assessment, valid and reliable data collection methods are at the heart of all evaluation efforts. As previously stressed, no single tool or technique can accurately represent an entire project. Just as delivery technologies grow more and more sophisticated, so too do technologies for assisting in evaluation. User logging and analysis used to be a monumental effort, even in multimedia systems. Now logging and analysis for basic website functions and other electronic systems can be handled efficiently with inexpensive software.

Above all, newly emerging evaluation technologies and techniques, like technology development in general, are migrating toward the support of collaboration, greater participation, and data sharing. Networked systems facilitate more reviewers at less cost, greater sharing, and, in turn, better utilization. The logistical challenges of getting data and reports into the hands of stakeholders are overcome, for example, by serving up-to-date documents from a single source. Through technology and shared networks, evaluation activities become integral components of the technological environment rather than isolated efforts.

Not all data collection issues—even those specifically related to evaluating electronic systems—have been met now that we have sophisticated monitoring and group networking tools. Challenges remain in those areas involving gathering representative responses from users and creating authentic representations of the user experience. Researchers and developers continue to search for better ways to measure and construct these key facets of the human-computer interface.

References

Dern, D. P. "Footprints and Fingerprints in Cyberspace: The Trail You Leave Behind." *Online,* July/August 1997, 44–50.

Geertz, C. "Thick Description: Toward an Interpretative Theory of Culture." In C. Geertz, *The Interpretation of Cultures.* New York: Basic Books, 1973, pp. 3–30.

Greene, J. C., and McClintock, C. "Triangulation in Evaluation: Design and Analysis Issues." *Evaluation Review,* 1985, *9,* 523–545.

Hilbert, D., and Redmiles, D. "Agents for Collecting Application Usage Data over the Internet." In *Agents '98: Proceedings of the Second International Conference on Autonomous Agents.* New York: Association for Computing Machinery, 1998, pp. 149–156.

Kilker, J., and Gay, G. "The Social Construction of a Digital Library: A Case Study Examining Implications for Evaluation." Information Technology and Libraries, 1998, pp. 60–70.

Marchionini, G., and Plaisant, C. *User Interface for the National Digital Library Program: Needs Assessment Report.* College Park, Maryland: Human-Computer Interaction Laboratory, University of Maryland at College Park, 1996.

Plaisant, C., Milash, B., Rose, A., Widoff, S., and Shneiderman, B. "Lifelines: Visualizing Personal Histories." In S. Card, J. Mackinlay, and B. Shneiderman (eds.), *Readings in Information Visualization: Using Vision to Think.* San Francisco: Morgan Kaufmann, 1999, pp. 287–294.

Trochim, W. "Concept Mapping." [http://trochim.human.cornell.edu/kb/conmap.htm]. June 25, 1999.

ROBERT H. RIEGER is assistant director of the Human-Computer Interaction Group in the department of communication at Cornell University.

AMANDA STURGILL is Radford Professor, department of journalism, Baylor University.

4

This chapter explores how multimedia records, particularly digital video, can enhance the analysis and presentation of research findings and can facilitate mixed-method research designs. The authors draw analogies between mixing methods and mixing technologies.

Using Multimedia Records to Support Mixed-Method Evaluation

Tammy L. Bennington, Geri Gay, Michael L. W. Jones

Innovations in electronic media have provided a variety of new tools and techniques to support evaluation activities. The ready availability and affordability of audio and video recording technologies make feasible the creation of multimedia technological records to supplement evaluation inquiry. Simultaneous developments in computer hardware and software that enable more efficient video digitization, compression, annotation and reproduction offer evaluators new analytical tools that feature multimedia data.

These developments in multimedia data have paralleled developments in the evaluation community regarding the potential benefits and challenges of mixing methods to support evaluation activities (for example, Caracelli and Greene, 1997; Datta, 1997). Drawing upon our experiences in collecting, analyzing, and presenting data encoded in diverse forms, we offer observations on the relationship between mixing methods and using multiple forms of data in evaluation.

This chapter investigates the benefits that can derive from the richness of multimedia data, particularly digitized video, and how the management, analysis, and presentation of that data can be facilitated by emerging software tools. We draw upon two examples of the use of multimedia data to facilitate evaluation research. The first study used quantitative data, transcripts, and video data, integrated through a customized multimedia spreadsheet, to facilitate interaction among evaluators examining the effectiveness of a collaborative learning environment. The second study used video records to complement an ethnographic study of the impact of computerization on a small middle school. Together, these studies illustrate some of the key benefits and challenges, as well as the potential, of using multimedia technological records in support of robust and holistic evaluation activities.

Mixed Media as Enabling Mixed Methods

Contemporary discussions of evaluation theory and practice have addressed the benefits and challenges of mixing various methods to achieve a broader and deeper understanding of social phenomena (see Greene and Caracelli, 1997). Although it appears intuitively evident that multiple approaches or methods applied to a given inquiry will yield more comprehensive or more nuanced understanding, numerous theoretical and pragmatic challenges ensue from attempts to integrate different methods of analysis into a coherent research strategy. In this section, we will provide a brief summary of the frameworks available for mixing methods and methodologies. We argue that these frameworks do not take into consideration how the relevance and contributions of a method are potentially transformed by the use of different technologies or media to implement or deliver the method. We explore how mixing technologies, and in particular using digital video, can enhance the strengths of mixed-methods approaches. We claim that they can do so by facilitating experimentation with the diverse characteristics of inquiry enumerated by Greene and Caracelli (1997), that is, by enabling greater or less particularity and generality or by fostering differential closeness or distance.

Mixed-method evaluation strategies aim to diffuse and even displace struggles between paradigms and approaches in evaluation work, such as those between quantitative versus qualitative methods, deduction versus induction, and molar versus molecular validity (Caracelli and Greene, 1997). Greene and Caracelli (1997) identify three stances or approaches to mixing inquiry paradigms in mixed-method evaluation: the purist, in which methods informed by different paradigms are viewed as fundamentally, epistemologically incompatible; the pragmatic, in which methods are mixed and fit to practical needs and concerns, with minimal concern for epistemological compatibility; and the dialectical, in which paradigmatic differences between methods are seen as providing tensions and contradictions from which new insights are derived. These latter two stances undergird different evaluation designs, which can be categorized, respectively, as component-centered or integrative (Caracelli and Greene, 1997).

The theoretical and practical challenges of mixing technologies in a loosely fitted mixed-technology component design or a tightly knit integrated design are analogous to those posed by the mixing of methods. As a component of a larger evaluation project, technologies such as digital audio and video can be used to provide complementary evidence for the observations and claims made by qualitative researchers; for example, providing video footage to support claims about interactional dynamics or emotional states, or as an independent objective source of corroborative evidence. Such records can also support triangulation among methods, since mediated records may contain details and patterns of interaction that are missed in traditional observation (Erickson, 1992). In addition, these technologies can facilitate more complex integrated mixed-method designs, such as with concept mapping.

As with mixing methods, mixing technologies entails mixing media that may encode different ways of knowing—for example, visual versus aural—with concomitant theoretical and epistemological implications for *how* one understands the information those media construct, for example, through visual interaction analysis or discourse analysis. Similarly, conducting a face-to-face interview recorded via notes and audiotape will produce a very different technological record than a computer-assisted personal interview recorded via ScreenCam™ and other tracking devices. Each record will afford different types of analysis and the production of different types of knowledge.

Technological records may also act as a primary data source that can be used to coordinate and integrate numerous evaluators' perspectives and analyses, as in the multimedia spreadsheet discussed below. Activity theory, presented earlier in this volume (Gay and Bennington), proposes that technological mediation be treated as a constitutive factor in evaluation practices. Technologies mediate human activity and as such are intrinsically constitutive of activity (Nardi, 1996) as well as of knowledge produced through and about the activity. It is arguable that within such a complex context, technologically mediated mixed-method evaluations should adopt an integrated mixed-method design so that the iterative engagement of different media enables new multidimensional and multivocal ways of using and understanding information. Many evaluation designs may not acknowledge that technological records mediate and contribute to evaluation in practice.

Tools for the Analysis and Integration of Multimedia Records

Capitalizing on the rich potential of digital video evaluation requires the use of specialized digital analysis tools explicitly designed around metaphors that treat video as a distinct form of data rather than a surrogate for written text. Continued technological innovation and the increased viability of using video in evaluation have afforded the development of many such tools (for example, Constellations, CEVA). Existing tools have also been redesigned (for example, MacSHAPA) to cope with the complexities of storing, indexing, classifying, marking, coding, annotating, and collaborating around video data asynchronously or in real time.

CEVA and MacSHAPA integrate video into analysis in a hybrid fashion, using VCRs to play analog video through the software interface. This hybrid solution does not afford the same degree of control and manipulation of video data as full digital video. However, it is often easier to set up and maintain and much less taxing on computing resources (Cockburn and Dale, 1997). What is intriguing about both packages is their ability to process and streamline video information in an accessible format that remains easy to navigate and explore without requiring extensive system resources. Both programs store and represent comments on video data via a timeline metaphor, thus preserving the temporal flow of video data. Video clips, still frames, and textual annotations are categorized and represented graphically, thereby allowing evaluators to quickly identify overlapping concepts and events that occur simultaneously. Arranging coding along conceptual and temporal lines affords not only strong qualitative analysis, but can also be useful in compiling descriptive quantitative statistical information. The CEVA database can be run over a network, allowing for multiple evaluators to analyze data simultaneously.

However, since each evaluator must share analog data on a distinct physical medium (the videocassette), synchronous collaboration in evaluation is difficult to coordinate effectively. Constellations (Figure 4.1), on the other hand, tightly integrates digital video into the analytical environment by displaying video files together with annotation fields and coding terms (Goldman-Segall, 1993).

Evaluators can record their observations and coding selections while the video selection plays simultaneously into the upper right quadrant of the screen. This allows the evaluator to see changes in coding in real time while simultaneously scanning the video for why such changes occurred— a valuable and efficient manner of reviewing coding procedures. The resulting post-analysis database consists of researcher notes and observations that are displayed synchronously with the flow of the video segment. Since the data source is digital, it is feasible to distribute the video over the network

Figure 4.1. Constellations

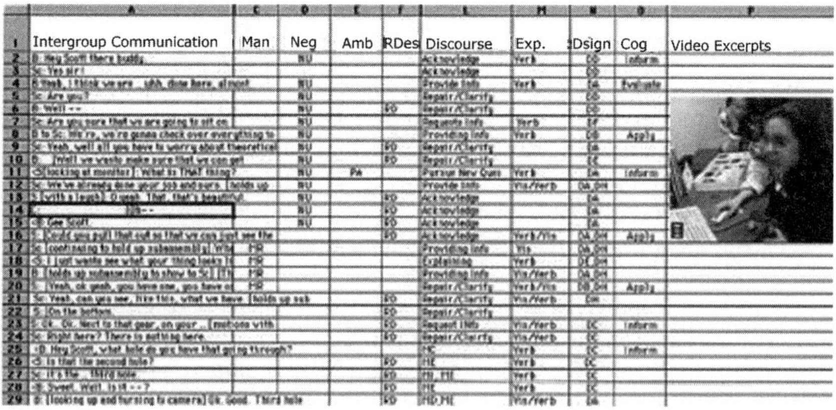

to other collaborators in evaluation. In its current form, however, Constellations does not afford true synchronous collaboration. A Web-based version of the software [http://www.webconstellations.com] is presently under development. This version deliberately targets evaluation contexts where distributed evaluators need to share a common data set simultaneously over the network.

Many of the challenges faced by researchers in the manipulation and analysis of digital video are similar to those faced by information specialists attempting to catalog video data and make them readily retrievable through video libraries. Video browsing and analysis software, such as CueVideo and VideoVISTA (Ponceleon and others, 1998), are currently being developed for library use. Another increasingly popular application of relevance to multimedia research is Folio Views, which allows hypertextual linking, annotation, multi-user access and extensive multimedia support through Microsoft Object Linking and Embedding (OLE) or through QuickTime™ movies.

Multimedia Evaluation in Practice: Two Examples

The benefits and limitations of such integrative technologies may be easier to illustrate through examples of actual uses. What follows is a brief overview of two cases in which multimedia technological records were used to support evaluation activities. The first, a study of the use of video-mediated communication to facilitate collaboration and task accomplishment in a college classroom, was primarily a mixed-method, mixed-media integrated design. It illustrates how mixed-media technological records can facilitate multidisciplinary, mixed-method collaborative evaluation. The second, a mixed-method component design evaluation of computerization at a middle school (which in practice became an integrative approach), used video data in conjunction with other methods to complement ethnographic analysis through triangulation. The background of each case will be described in some detail to inform subsequent discussion of specific findings and limitations that emerged from the evaluation process.

Case Study One: Multimedia Spreadsheet Tool. In the first case study, we used video-based interaction analysis to evaluate students' interactions and use of information resources as they collaborated on a required design project in an undergraduate engineering class. The students were given the task of constructing a wind-driven device capable of charging a two-volt battery. Groups of students collaborated from a distance via a prototype computer-mediated communication system that allowed the separated groups to share drawings and text on the computer screens. The purpose of the exercise was to determine how the students' collaborative design efforts could be supported by the system.

The activities of the groups were videotaped. Video provides a rich, thickly detailed visual and aural record and is an appropriate tool for observing group behavior in a naturalistic setting. We tried to limit the major drawbacks of video, that is, a constrained field of view and limited record of human sensory data, by carefully organizing the workspace setup. The cameras monitored the group members, their work area, and the computer screen used for database searching and drawing. Microphones captured both inter-and intragroup conversations. Because the students in our setup were intensely focused on their work, they rapidly became habituated to the presence of the video cameras, only acknowledging the cameras' presence when explicitly communicating with the other groups.

The entire video record was transcribed and entered into an Excel™ spreadsheet. Use of resources and tools by the design groups was also entered into the spreadsheet by time initiated and duration. In addition, two evaluators selected portions of the videotapes to be digitized as QuickTime™ movies and added the digital video segments to the spreadsheet. The integrated data in the spreadsheet was used by an interdisciplinary team of evaluators to coordinate feedback and comments. Multiple evaluators could access the data and submit their analyses or commentary to the collective data source (Figure 4.2).

Figure 4.2 shows how the spreadsheet was used to accommodate multiple data formats and allow for cross-referencing of text and digitized video (Gay and Mazur, 1993). Column A contained the written transcript of interactions seen in the video. Columns B and G (hidden) contained coding of inter-and intragroup communication, respectively. Columns C through F and Column L contained discourse-centered coding, Column N design coding, and Column O cognitive coding. Excerpts from video data were inserted at

Figure 4.2. An Example of the Multimedia Spreadsheet in Use

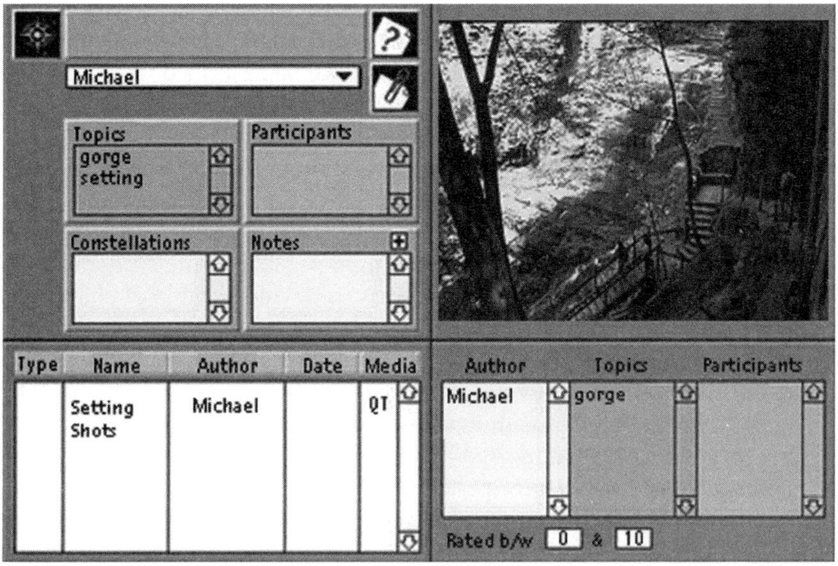

the appropriate points in Column P. By a process of progressive refinement (Roschelle and Goldman, 1991), the video record was pared down in an iterative fashion to target specific instances deemed representative of the entire context. These clips were selected to accompany and strategically elaborate the full transcript presented in the multimedia spreadsheet. The completed spreadsheet was uploaded to an Internet server to facilitate coding and commentary by multiple evaluators.

Case Study Two: Multimedia Records Supporting Ethnographic Analysis in a School Setting. The second case study used video recording to complement a formative study on computerization at a small private middle school (grades seven through nine) (Jones, 1998). The school had received four computers and a high-speed Internet connection to serve as a field test site for mathematics educational software. Since the full-time presence of computers at the school was a new phenomenon, educators, evaluators, and software developers alike agreed that it would be interesting to see how students and teachers adapted to the presence of this new technological infrastructure.

The evaluation group planned an ethnographic study as a preliminary phase to field testing the software in question. Whereas the first phase was primarily descriptive in nature, the second was explicitly formative, aiming to solicit information that would inform later iterations of the software and, more generally, illuminate how computer software and hardware could facilitate mathematics instruction in this setting.

These two distinct but complementary goals influenced how methods and media were combined to inform analysis. In both phases of the study, video records were primarily used to validate data obtained from observational field notes. In practice, however, video records were used in a more integrated fashion, informing and informed by field notes in a mutually constitutive fashion. The more explicit focus on systemic change in the second phase added a normative and change-oriented element to the evaluation. The convergence of multiple forms of data was useful in providing justifications for recommended changes.

In the first phase, video recordings were transcribed in full. The resulting transcriptions were analyzed in conjunction with researcher notes on field visits and administrative meetings via the qualitative content analysis software NUD*IST. In the second phase, time and budgetary restrictions limited the potential for such a robust analysis. Evaluation in this phase was based on field notes that were annotated by iterative reviews of video records.

Contributions of Multimedia Records to Evaluation

The use of video records greatly facilitated the evaluation activities in both cases. Video records supported mixed-method analysis by allowing the convergence of multiple forms and representations of data, providing a flexible and relatively rich record of events, and allowing analysis to occur asynchronously, collaboratively, and from diverse locations.

The Convergence of Multiple Forms and Representations of Data

In both cases, video proved to be an excellent means of supporting other evaluation methods. The multimedia spreadsheet afforded the juxtapositioning and even convergence of multiple forms of data, both quantitative and qualitative. Video records and their resulting transcripts were accompanied by quantitative tracking data and the comments and coding of other evaluators working on the project (see Figure 4.2). Each of these data sources would provide a useful but partial sense of what transpired if analyzed independently from one another. The juxtapositioning enabled by the multimedia spreadsheet facilitated comparisons among different kinds of mediated data, analytical codes, and researchers' codings and comments; it made potential contradictions more readily identifiable, thus facilitating a more integrated, dialectical evaluation process. It enabled more complex representations of the relationships in and among data, including the simultaneous representation of the particular and the general, the unusual and the representative, the micro and the macro (Greene and Caracelli, 1997).

The convergence of multiple methods in a single visual display revealed various activities that evaluators had previously missed. Designers of the collaborative system in the first example had noticed from computer usage statistics that participants did not heavily use the knowledge management database. The designers were concerned to identify any technical faults that could be redressed in later versions. Video recordings of interaction with the system showed, however, that participants were willing to use the database, but found that text and voice communication over the network was easier and better supported the task at hand. This observation had eluded designers and researchers until the video record had been collected and analyzed. The convergence of on-line tracking information, video data, and transcripts helped reconstruct elements of the full usage context and helped evaluators uncover the situated dynamics of use. Multiple representations, each offering their own distinct impression of events, recreated the context of use and assisted evaluators' interpretations and negotiations of meaning (Gay and Mazur, 1993).

In the school ethnography, video was primarily used as an independent and secondary support for observational methods. For example, teachers attempted to use collaborative knowledge databases as a means of coordinating and publishing group projects. These databases also proved to be underutilized in practice, since students found it much easier to communicate using face-to-face interaction, written notes, and printouts of computer work. Ethnographic observations were key in uncovering what off-camera activity was transpiring in order to complete collaborative projects. However, the video record offered extensive and detailed information regarding student patterns of human-computer interaction, by recording how students used the computers as well as screen content and the tasks in which they were involved. Used in tandem with human observation, the video record proved instrumental in reconstructing a full, rich description of activity and context.

Multimedia Records as a Relatively Rich and Malleable Information Source. Multimedia records are especially useful tools to represent the dynamics of action and interaction within a given context. The simultaneous integration of detailed visual imagery, motion, and audio gives video data a sense of wholeness and richness that other technological records such as audiotape cannot provide. As such, video creates a powerful impression of familiarity, intimacy, and credibility that can be used to defend and justify qualitative observations and knowledge claims, add texture and context to quantitative data, and serve as a proxy for researcher observation when necessary.

Video is also a very accessible, engaging, and familiar representation. The low conceptual overhead of video data collection may make the evaluation process more accessible to all involved stakeholders. For example, in the school ethnography, findings from both phases of the study were presented to the class in two debriefing sessions. The first session was a face-to-face discussion with no supporting audiovisual material. While the session overall was productive and engaging, it took some time for the evaluator to initiate discussion and, once begun, it was somewhat difficult to keep the discussion on topic. The second debriefing began with a presentation of video data from the year's observations. The twenty-minute tape was an engaging and entertaining vehicle to spur conversation and discussion, and it provided a common focus around which future discussions could be structured.

Video records can also be a very fluid and malleable medium to analyze when converted into digital form (Goldman-Segall, 1998). Digital video can be scanned quickly and at various speeds, stored in multiple formats, duplicated rapidly, and shipped between users with ease via computer networks. Streaming video technologies offer a range of possibilities for storing, streaming, and integrating video into web sites, spreadsheets, and applications tailored to meet researcher needs. Emblaze, RealMedia, QuickTime, and MS Media Player support diverse forms of video and audio presentation, including live broadcasts (Media Player).

Digital video is also relatively easy to splice into sections, edit, and reconstitute into compilations and alternate sequences. This is especially useful in video data analysis, where it is often pragmatically unfeasible to transcribe and analyze long videotaped sessions. Evaluators using video data tend to use representative video sequences that succinctly portray key points, and subject those sections to detailed analysis (for example, Bødker, 1996; Nardi, 1996). Such reduction is necessary to make the prospect of using video records in evaluation plausible. The time-intensive nature of video analysis is discussed in greater depth below.

Video Data in Support of Collaboration over Space and Time. In the first example, evaluators took advantage of the capacity of video records to transcend spatial and temporal constraints of real-time, on-site inquiry (Hartson, Castillo, Kelso, and Neale, 1996). Evaluators were able to investigate and annotate the records at their own pace, skim over some interactions in favor of others, and continually revisit key sequences if necessary. Distributing the data set over the Internet allowed evaluators to conduct their analyses at a distance from the evaluation setting. Although it may be advisable in theory to have video records complement on-site evaluator observation, it may be pragmatically unfeasible to do so, especially in cases such as this, where a number of evaluators from different disciplines and different organizations participate in analysis. Involving all six evaluators in on-site activities would have probably influenced the nature of social interactions that were observed and recorded.

The use of multimedia records greatly facilitated the integration of multiple perspectives and areas of expertise as well as interaction among evaluators with different areas of expertise. The engineering evaluators in particular noted that the juxtapositioning of qualitative and quantitative data and the use of multimedia records to represent qualitative research findings strongly corresponded to established practices in representing information in their discipline. Moreover, such tools can facilitate participatory and transformative evaluation through enabling collaborative analysis among evaluators and stakeholders. Juxtaposing different points of view, codings of data, and annotations of visual and verbal texts can reveal patterns, discrepancies, and convergences to produce new insights into phenomena under study. Collaborative viewing and collaborative analysis can facilitate understanding and learning among evaluators and stakeholders as they engage with each other through the data.

Potential Limitations of the Use of Multimedia Records in Evaluation

The use of multimedia technologies to record situated interactions proved to be largely beneficial in both of the above examples. However, the reader may have noted that some of the benefits described above would have undesirable consequences that could frustrate the evaluation process if not adequately anticipated and controlled. These include problems with interpreting visual technological records as necessarily "real," ethical concerns specific to the use of video, and the complex nature of multimedia data analysis.

Video data are often touted as a rich, high-fidelity form of representation. Such benefits are often preceded or followed by qualifications and examples that remind us not to subscribe to a naive realist position with respect to video representations (Harper, 1998; see also Gay and Bennington, this volume). While videotaping does offer a reasonably faithful though partial representation of actions and interactions in context, the resultant record is still very much dependent on various creative factors such as selective attention, camera placement, enframing, focus, lighting conditions, background-foreground distinctions, and the interference of off-camera audio (Issacs and Tang, 1996). The partiality of the resulting data set would have to be acknowledged and addressed as a mediating factor in analysis. Awareness of the constructedness and partiality of video data can be heightened through techniques such as disrupting the fluidity of camera movement with jerky movements and uneven focus, or by incorporating critical aural commentary or narration into the video. These issues draw attention to the critical literacy skills necessary for the competent and responsible use and consumption of multimedia technologies (see below).

As Bennington notes in the final chapter of this volume, the storage and use of digitized video records in the presentation of research findings pose challenges to traditionally held expectations of privacy, anonymity, and confidentiality. Digital video representations can be sent over the network and copied with ease. This raises interesting challenges regarding access and security for digital images. Figure 4.2 of the multimedia spreadsheet, discussed earlier in this chapter, is an excellent case in point. As per common practice, transcripts of talk are made anonymous so that individuals cannot be identified. Digital video also affords the easy concealment of identity by using still image or video editing software to mask regions of the image.

The complexity and quantity of video data contribute to particular difficulties in analysis. Fully transcribing video proves to be a monotonous and time-consuming process, taking approximately six hours per hour of raw footage (Jones, 1998). Video transcription is particularly complex, since audio transcriptions should be accompanied by representations of imagery and motion. As noted above, video data are often spliced into small sections to facilitate analysis. This process can be quite complex, involving a series of educated guesses, judgment calls, and selections shaped by researcher interpretations. Video may in some cases present ambiguity in voice attributions. While audio and motion imagery are integrated in video recordings, it does not necessarily follow that they are synchronized perfectly (Issacs and Tang, 1996). The video lens is trained on one specific direction, and does not record interactions that lay outside its preset bounds. Microphones, however, tend to pick up both immediate and ambient sounds, such as other conversations occurring off camera. Transcribers and analysts who are not intimately familiar with the actors and dynamics of the context of study may find it impossible to determine the origin and meaning of audio emerging from off-screen participants.

Analysis of digital video data can also be somewhat crippled given current limitations in computer hardware and software. Although more recent consumer-grade desktop computers are powerful enough to process video data, substantial editing and post-processing requires a large amount of processing power, lots of disk storage, and video editing and annotation software. Distributing video data of any substantial size over computer networks requires high-speed network connections, thus limiting the portability of such data sets. Moreover, existing qualitative analysis tools (for example, NUD*IST, HyperQual, Inspiration, FolioViews, Atlas/ti) continue to privilege text-based records over multimedia inputs. Though later versions of these text-centered utilities can accept video and audio data, the programs are not well suited to engage this data in further, in-depth analysis. NUD*IST, for example, integrates nontext records as unitary documents that can be coded as a whole yet cannot be dissected within the program.

Evaluators in the first example used a spreadsheet to coordinate data analysis and management. The spreadsheet was a quite satisfactory interim solution, as it could contain and display numerous forms of data simultaneously. Unlike programs with more hard-wired design constraints, the spreadsheet provides a relatively flexible environment that affords a degree of customization regarding the input, handling, and editing of data. That said, it would still be preferable to use analysis software that is designed explicitly to contain and represent multimedia records and that enables in-depth analysis of multimedia data through annotation and segmentation.

The Need for a New Multimedia Literacy

Integrating digital video as a unique representational form and source of information into evaluation inquiry can facilitate the process identified by Greene and Caracelli (1997) of creating an alternative set of inquiry characteristics that enable attention to a plurality of voices and perspectives. The incorporation of digital video into the collection, analysis, and presentation of data can contribute to highlighting and learning from the tensions between particularity and generality, closeness and distance, contextualized local meanings and the distanced identification of regularities. Effectively using digital video records for such purposes, however, requires the development of a new kind of literacy among evaluators—multimedia or metamedia literacy (Lemke, 1998).

As noted above, researchers can learn visual and compositional techniques that can facilitate the exploration of tensions among inquiry characteristics as methods and media are integrated. The organization of multimedia data and the composition of its presentation can provide analytical insight as well as contribute to the construction of innovative and provocative meanings through the juxtapositioning of multimedia representations, the use of hypertext to link and navigate data sets in nonlinear ways, aural annotation, and the intimate incorporation of video into textual data, as in the multimedia, collaborative spreadsheet discussed above. Multimedia technologies thereby provide new metaphors around which to organize both the analysis and presentation of data—topological, rhizomic, three-dimensional immersive, and so forth. Digital video can provide zooming capabilities that allow visual access to different levels of analysis, as well as complex, emergent representations of the unusual and the representative (Greene and Caracelli, 1997). However, this literacy also entails recognizing the limitations of different forms of data embodiment and representation.

Conclusion

The potential of digital multimedia records and analytical tools to support mixed-method evaluation depends on recognizing that methods are mediated by technologies and that different technologies produce qualitatively different data and different mediated representations of the phenomena they record. The different media and technologies used to collect, organize, analyze, and represent data provide different affordances for evaluation activities and affect the kinds of knowledge claims that can be produced.

Digitized multimedia records can

- Provide relatively rich, multidimensional and multilevel representations of actions and interactions, as well as contexts
- Integrate numerous forms of data to support integrated media and integrated method evaluation
- Facilitate data analysis by affording ease of selection, editing, splicing, juxtaposing, and clustering of diverse media
- Foster new insights by facilitating the identification of patterns, contradictions, and disjunctions through juxtapositioning media and through enabling collaborative, multidimensional, and hypertextual analysis
- Enable flexible, nonlinear engagement with data through coding, hyperlinks, and random access technologies
- Facilitate quantitative analysis of the frequency or duration of occurrences or behaviors, while simultaneously allowing qualitative annotation of the video record to fill out the analysis
- Support collaborative and distanced interactions, even dialogues, among evaluators who may not be present at the site of the evaluation project
- Facilitate, through collaborative spaces and tools, participatory evaluation by enabling stakeholders to engage in data analysis and provide commentary

Multimedia technologies, including digital video, mediate these analytical activities. As many contemporary treatments of technology note, these technologies are not neutral. They shape, even constitute, the way we encounter and understand the world. They mediate methods, methodologies, and paradigmatic approaches to research and evaluation. Reflection on how they do this needs to be acknowledged and incorporated into ongoing discussions of mixed-methods approaches.

References

Bødker, S. "Applying Activity Theory to Video Analysis: How to Make Sense of Video Data in Human-Computer Interaction." In B. Nardi (ed.), *Context and Consciousness.* Cambridge, Mass.: MIT Press, 1996.

Caracelli, V. J., and Greene, J. C. "Crafting Mixed-Method Evaluation Designs." In J. C. Greene and V. J. Caracelli (eds.), *Advances in Mixed-Method Evaluation: The Challenges and Benefits of Integrating Diverse Paradigms.* New Directions in Evaluation, no. 74. San Francisco: Jossey-Bass, 1997.

Cockburn, A., and Dale, T. "CEVA: A Tool for Collaborative Video Analysis." *Proceedings of the ACM GROUP97 Conference.* New York: Association for Computing Machinery, 1997.

Datta, L. "A Pragmatic Basis for Mixed-Method Designs." In J. C. Greene and V. J. Caracelli (eds.), *Advances in Mixed-Method Evaluation: The Challenges and Benefits of Integrating Diverse Paradigms*. New Directions in Evaluation, no.74. San Francisco: Jossey-Bass, 1997.

Erickson, F. "Ethnographic Microanalysis of Interaction." In M. LeCompte, W. Millroy, and J. Preissle (eds.), *The Handbook of Qualitative Research in Education*. San Diego: Academic Press, 1992.

Gay, G. K., and Mazur, J. "The Utility of Computer Tracking Tools for User-Centered Design." *Educational Technology*, 1993, 34 (3), 45–59.

Goldman-Segall, R. (1993). "Interpreting Video Data. Journal for Educational Multimedia and Hypermedia." *Association for the Advancement of Computing in Education*, 1993, 2 (3), 261–282.

Goldman-Segall, R. *Points of Viewing Children's Thinking: A Digital Ethnographer's Journey*. Mahwah, N.J.: Erlbaum, 1998.

Greene, J. C., and Caracelli, V. J. "Defining and Describing the Paradigm Issue in Mixed-Method Evaluation." In J. C. Greene and V. J. Caracelli (eds.), *Advances in Mixed-Method Evaluation: The Challenges and Benefits of Integrating Diverse Paradigms*. New Directions for Evaluation, no. 74. San Francisco: Jossey-Bass, 1997.

Harper, D. "On the Authority of the Image: Visual Methods at the Crossroads." In N. Denzin and Y. Lincoln (eds.), *Collecting and Interpreting Qualitative Materials*. Thousand Oaks, Calif.: Sage, 1998.

Hartson, H. R., Castillo, J. C., Kelso, J., and Neale, W. C. "Remote Evaluation: The Network as an Extension of the Usability Laboratory." *CHI '96. Conference Proceedings on Human Factors in Computing Systems*. Vancouver, British Columbia, April, 1996.

Issacs, E. A., and Tang, J. C. "Studying Video-Based Collaboration in Context: From Small Workgroups to Large Organizations." In K. E. Finn, A. J. Sellen, and S. B. Wilbur (eds.), *Video-Mediated Communication*. Mahwah, N.J.: Erlbaum, 1996.

Jones, M. L. W. "Where Do You Want to Go Tomorrow? Shaping Alternative Technological Futures via Ethnographically Informed Participatory Design." Unpublished master's thesis, School of Communication, Simon Fraser University, 1998.

Lemke, J. L. "Metamedia Literacy: Transforming Meanings and Media." In D. Reinking (ed.), *Handbook of Literacy and Technology: Transformations in a Post-Typographic World*. Mahwah, N.J.: Erlbaum, 1998.

Nardi, B. A. "Studying Context: A Comparison of Activity Theory, Situated Action Models, and Distributed Cognition." In B. Nardi (ed.), *Context and Consciousness* . Cambridge, Mass.: MIT Press, 1996.

Ponceleon, D., Srinivason, S., Amir, A., Petkovic, D., and Diklic, D. "Key to Effective Video Retrieval: Effective Cataloging and Browsing." *ACM Multimedia '98*, 1998, 99–106.

Roschelle, J., and Goldman, S. "VideoNoter: A Productivity Tool for Video Data Analysis." *Behavior Research Methods, Instruments and Computers*, 1991, 23, 219–224.

TAMMY L. BENNINGTON is research associate in the Human-Computer Interaction Group at Cornell University and adjunct professor in the Program on Social and Organizational Learning at George Mason University.

GERI GAY is associate professor in the department of communications at Cornell University and director of the Human-Computer Interaction Group at Cornell.

MICHAEL L. W. JONES is a doctoral candidate in the department of communications at Cornell University.

5

Verbal protocols constitute a useful tool for evaluating computer hardware and software, especially if informed by activity theory, although they cannot stand alone in a thorough evaluation design.

Using Verbal Protocol Methodology in the Evaluation of Software and Hardware

Sandra Mathison, Tricia R. Meyer, Juan D. Vargas[1]

Much of the evaluation of technology focuses on outcomes and favors data collection strategies such as surveys, standardized student achievement measures, and attitude measures (see, for example, Baker, Gearhart, and Herman, 1994; Kulik, 1994; Mitra and Hullett, 1997). Additionally, a substantial literature emphasizes the use of checklists for rating surface features of software and hardware to aid in adoption decisions (see, for example, Blease, 1986).

Evaluations that focus on process tend to be formative in nature, often in the context of alpha and beta testing of software, that is, when software is in the early stages of development and for debugging software that is near completion (Flagg, 1990). Flagg (1990) suggests a range of data collection strategies to be used if the purpose is to "inform decisions about design, production, and implementation" (p. 23). These strategies include diaries, logs, think-aloud protocols, escorted trials, confederates, questionnaires, interviews, expert review, and focus groups. This broad array of data collection methods is consistent with Johnston's caution that case studies and field trials, rather than experiments and summative designs, are most useful for the evaluation of information technologies (Johnston, 1984). There is a trend for developing electronic-based instruments as the primary data collection strategy. These can be in the form of electronic surveys (see, for example, Pariset, 1990) or outcome measures, such as the creation of a hypercard stack as an indicator of students' understanding (Baker, Niemi, and Herl, 1994).

New Directions for Evaluation, no. 84, Winter 1999 © Jossey-Bass Publishers

Verbal protocol is a methodology, among others, that is used in the evaluation of computer software and hardware, although most often in formative evaluations. Simply put, verbal protocol is a data collection technique that asks the user-consumer to talk aloud while interacting with the technology, thus revealing the cognitive processes of the user. Even though verbal protocols are increasingly used, there are a number of cautions. Flagg (1990) points out the obtrusiveness of the researcher, the restriction on the technique with those not especially verbally able, and the limits it presents with younger children. These constraints are, in part, based on the underlying philosophical perspective, namely, that of information processing theory. However, we will suggest that adopting an activity theory perspective eliminates these constraints and suggests significant advantages. The primary advantage of verbal protocols is they provide data on learners' cognitive processes and responses that otherwise would be investigated only indirectly (Pressley and Afflerbach, 1995). Verbal protocols examine the relationship among thought, language, and performance. Pressley and Afflerbach (1995) caution that the growing popularity of verbal protocol analysis notwithstanding, it should not be seen as a "mature" methodology, but rather one requiring careful thought and much more refinement.

This chapter very briefly discusses the history of verbal protocols, which is long and rich, and examines the most common philosophical orientation to verbal protocols—a theory of information processing. We also challenge this common orientation by explicating the use of verbal protocols within a different theoretical orientation—a cultural-historical activity theory (CHAT). A story of using verbal protocols in evaluation which evolved from an information processing theory perspective to the CHAT perspective, will weave these more theoretical discussions together.

Historical Context of Verbal Protocols

Ericsson and Simon (1993) note that early speculations about the human mind and human subjective experiences were in the form of religious and philosophical questions about the nature of humankind. The human mind was generally viewed as beyond scientific understanding. However, individual philosophers inquired about how to obtain new knowledge and the nature of correspondence between the external world and subjective experience. Aristotle and Plato were known for encouraging people to talk about what was on their minds, seeking general issues about how the mind functions.

William James (1890) used introspection, or subjects' reports of their thinking—including speculation about actions, reasons for actions, and narratives of how to carry out action—to develop psychological theory. Introspection became the basis for psychology, and self-observation became the means to understanding the mind. The validity of introspection is based on the notion that people are capable and to be trusted and, what is more important, that everyone will self-evidently understand each utterance (Tichener, 1920).

Of course, the value of introspection did not go unchallenged. Watson (1913) claimed that introspection created interference—self-reports not only included the contents of one's short-term memory but also embody the theories of mind through reflectiveness and digression. Hence, he concluded, introspection was inadequate knowledge upon which to build theories of cognitive processing (Pressley and Afflerbach, 1995). Instead, Watson suggested that "a good deal more can be learned about the psychology of thinking by making subjects think aloud about definite problems, than by trusting to the unscientific method of introspection" (Watson, 1920, p. 91).

These early forays into the mind were sidelined by the dominance of behaviorism in the 1960s. Behaviorists and behavioral theory did not need cognition, the focus was on overt performance, not mediating processes (Ericsson and Simon, 1993). The use of verbal protocols waned.

Information Processing Theory and Verbal Protocols

Information processing (IP) theory compares cognition to computer modeling to account for the ways people process, store, and retrieve information. The goal of IP researchers is to build models of cognitive processes based on verbal reports that will predict the unfolding of future verbal reports (Ericsson and Simon, 1993). IP's purpose thus lies in "developing and testing detailed processing models of cognition, models that can often be formalized in computer programming languages and analyzed by a computer simulation" (Ericsson and Simon, 1993, p. 220).

IP theory focuses on both long-term and short-term memory. Long-term memory contains knowledge of how to do things (that is, procedural knowledge) as well as factual knowledge (that is, declarative knowledge). Some knowledge is episodic in that it is a memory of some specific event in the thinker's life (for instance, recollection of attending a Rolling Stones concert). Other knowledge is more generalized, not tied to specific events, but representative of types of events in general (for example, knowledge of what goes on at a rock concert). The most important characteristic of long-term memory is its huge information capacity; fortunately the information is organized. People differ in the degree and kind of organization of their long-term memory. For any individual, some types of information will be more organized than other types of information (Pressley and Afflerbach, 1995).

Short-term memory, on the other hand, derives from two sources: immediate experience, and associations of that experience to information stored in long-term memory. If you see a person for the first time and then close your eyes to imagine that individual, short-term memory calls on stimulation from external sensations. You then begin to think about other people who look like this individual; new names and faces enter short-term memory, associations that come from long-term memory.

A key element in the use of verbal protocols is that people can actually identify information in short-term memory. From the information reported, the evaluator can make inferences about problem-solving processes. An utterance therefore serves as a trace, a course of evidence, through which to infer the inner workings of the mind. Consider Ericsson and Simon's (1980) characterization of a "verbal report": "With the instruction to verbalize, a direct trace is obtained of the heeded information, and hence, an indirect one of the internal stages of the cognitive process" (p. 220). They continue, "Within the context of this general model, verbalization processes produce [externalize] information that is in [short-term memory]" (p. 220). Thinking aloud, they conclude, "will not change the structure and course of the task processes, although it may slightly decrease the speed of task performance" (p. 226). Verbalizations "involve either direct articulation of information stored in a language (verbal code, Level 1 verbalization); articulation of verbal recoding of non-propositional information without additional processing (Level 2 verbalization); or articulation after scanning, filtering, inference, or generative processes have modified the information available (Level 3 verbalization)" (p. 227). People can, they conclude, simply dump the contents of their short-term memory.

IP theorists recognize, however, that contextual factors may influence verbalizations. "Various kinds of intermediate processes may intervene between the internal representation of information and its verbalization . . . and . . . [the] circumstances under which verbalization takes place can have a significant effect on what is verbalized and on the interpretation of the verbal data" (Ericsson and Simon, 1980, p. 218). As a consequence, the use of verbal protocols within this theoretical tradition requires the use of carefully crafted instructions provided by evaluators to cue particular reports from participants, that is, cues that will direct retrieval of specific bits of information from short-term memory.

The verbal protocol therefore is a report of short-term memory that is elicited with as little specific direction as possible. The creation of a verbal protocol is not an act of communication (Ericsson and Simon, 1993); instead, "the experimental situation is arranged to make clear that social interaction is not intended, and the experimenter is seated behind (not visible to) the subject. . . . social interaction between subject and experimenter is then minimized" (p. xiv). Prompts from the researcher should be along the lines of "keep talking" because such prompts are least directive and do not suggest the need for a direct answer to the researcher (p. 256). Interaction should be minimized to the greatest extent possible to elicit pure cognitive processes.

Other cognitive theorists have noted that the act of composing a verbal response may result in the development of new ideas, especially during ill-structured tasks (Bracewell and Breuleux, 1994). Ericsson and Simon (1980) suggest that such insights are not discoveries, but rather reflect a certain sort of memory retrieval. What appears to be a sudden insight is really the retrieval of prior knowledge that is brought to bear on a new problem, a reorganization of information from memory into new schemata.

Ericsson and Simon (1993, p. 61) suggest some ongoing problems with verbal protocols:

- The subject's cognitive processes change when the subject talks and thinks at the same time.
- The subject may not verbalize all that is running through his or her mind.
- Verbalizations may report some irrelevant, yet parallel, thought process occurring in one's mind.

The list below summarizes the main features of the IP and CHAT (which will be described more fully later) perspectives for contrast purposes.

Information Processing Theory (IP)	Cultural Historical Activity Theory (CHAT)
Purpose: develop models of cognitive processing	Purpose: understand how speech represents and mediates knowledge and learning
Concerned with solitary constructed thought	Concerned with socially constructed thought
Neutralizes confounding factors	Acknowledges and uses all factors
Concerned with pure, clean thought	Concerned with mutually constructed thought
Ideas are developed spontaneously, cued by instructions	Ideas are developed through negotiations with evaluator, past experiences, values, beliefs
Training of evaluators and participants is essential	Training of evaluators and participants not necessary
Uses clear scripted instructions for uniform interactions with participants	Fosters nonuniform interactions with participants
Minimal interaction between evaluator and participant	Dependent on interaction between evaluator and participant
Provides a window into participants' mind	Provides understanding of a social context

Case Example: Reading the Web

The Reading the Web project is exploring how people reason with and from hypermedia text (including hypertext, graphics, and embedded video) and is examining whether this reasoning is different from that employed with print text and whether there is anything to be learned about differences in reasoning for novices and experts.[2] At the outset of the project it was unclear how the research should proceed, although there was a shared interest in observing people's behavior while reading on the Web, rather than, for example, looking at outcome measures such as performance on other tasks in conjunction with Reading the Web. The question that focused the earlier stages of this project was, How do adult students search, interact with, make sense of, and value the information contained on pages of the World Wide Web (WWW)? (Swan and others, 1998, p. 96).

The project adopted a think-aloud protocol methodology, although this was combined with other data collection strategies, including demographics of participants, video taping of participants' faces and the computer screen, and stimulated recall. The authors describe their methodology further:

> Subjects were asked to spend one-half hour researching the general topic of "electronic literacy," bookmarking the items they found particularly useful, and thinking aloud as they did so. Specifically, they were asked to "dump" the contents of their short-term memory as they worked, but not to reflect on what they were doing or why (in accordance with procedures modeled by the researchers and practiced by the subjects). Instead, subjects' reflections on their activities were captured after the subjects had completed their searches [by] using a stimulate recall procedure. [Swan and others, 1998, p. 97]

The actual script of the verbal protocol for the Reading the Web project is reproduced in the extract below. It illustrates a number of characteristics tying this research project primarily to an IP perspective: the choice of a simple isolated task that participants did not assist in creating, the minimal interaction between the participants and the evaluator, the focus on short-term memory "dumping," the clear separation of data from thinking aloud with reflection or introspection.

Instructions to Subjects

In this study, we're interested in videotaping how people use the Internet, and what they are thinking as they work. We'll be asking you to talk aloud as you work and afterwards we would like to ask you some questions as we view parts of the videotape together.

First, we have some forms to fill out [the personal information and consent and release forms].

Okay, let's get started. [Hand them a copy of the task and go over with them and allow them to ask for clarifications. Next describe the talk aloud procedures.]

We'd like you to talk aloud as you complete the task we are going to give you. We'd like to hear everything that goes through your mind, including anything you might be reading from the screen, even if it is irrelevant. Don't plan or edit what you're saying. We're going to ask you to continue talking all the time. Otherwise, we will remind you to keep talking.

[While subjects are browsing, remember to take notes and jot down questions for the recall portion. Stop subjects after half hour. When finished, say, Now let's look at the tape together and talk about it.]

In the Reading the Web study, the tapes were transcribed, coded, and recoded (for inter-rater reliability) for patterns of behavior, although in fact the data analysis favored the think-aloud data, a preference that was evidenced throughout the planning and data collection phases of the project. From the analysis of the verbal protocols, the study concluded that subject domain knowledge (electronic literacy), Internet experience, and characteristics of the WWW "text" (including content, design, and layout) were relevant factors for how participants read the Web. Additionally, "all subjects seemed to pursue unique strategies for finding and making sense of information that somehow mirrored ways in which they related to the world and their general experiences in it" (Swan and others, 1998, p. 98).

This study concludes with the development of a model of reading on the WWW, offering another link to the IP perspective. This model mirrors how IP theorists see the short-term memory, accessed through the verbal protocol, as a window to long-term memory and especially stored prior experiences. One could assume that in following this approach, a next stage in the research might be to develop the model further by accounting for the dimensionality of various factors, such as differences between expert and novice Internet users. Further, the authors suggest that refinement of the task is critical to making it transparent, so that the task will elicit "natural reading behaviors" (p. 100).

We will discuss the refocusing of the research, cast in the context of activity theory, after we describe how activity theory differs from IP, especially with regard to the use of verbal protocols.

Cultural Historical Activity Theory and Verbal Protocols

Cultural-historical activity theory (CHAT) presents an alternative framework to information processing theory—one is more informative if one is interested in judging the quality of either software or hardware. This section outlines the features of CHAT and is followed by a continuation of the case example, a project that has been substantially enhanced through a conceptual shift from IP to CHAT.

CHAT is informed by a number of theorists (Bahktin, 1985; Cole, 1992; Cole, Engeström, and Vasquez, 1997; Leont'ev, 1976; Vygotsky, 1987; Wertsch, 1991) working in the "three-fold historical origins in classical German philosophy (from Kant to Hegel), in the writing of Marx and Engels, and in the Soviet Russian cultural-historical psychology of Vygotsky, Leont'ev, and Luria" (Engström, 1999, p. 20). Activity theory is based on the social nature of developing thoughts rather than in predicting the production of them. Vygotsky (1987) suggests that human consciousness is not made up of isolated single minds but that there is a *social mind,* the structure and function of which is predicated on how a person has learned to use cultural tools. The mind is therefore created—socially, culturally, historically.

Vygotsky (1987) further posits that understanding *cognition*—sense making—is dependent on speech, the analysis of words, but not words in isolation. For Bahktin (1985), utterances achieve meaning as part of a greater whole in which there is a constant interaction among meanings, whereas Wertsch (1991) makes the claim that an utterance reflects not only the voice producing it, but also the voices to which it is addressed. In other words, the formulation of an utterance responds in some way to previous utterances and anticipates the responses of other, succeeding ones. When it is understood (is meaningful), an utterance comes into contact with the "counter word" of those who hear it (Smagorinsky, 1998). The social role of speech is based on Vygotsky's notion of egocentric speech modified by Cole's (1992, 1996) critique of Vygotsky's insufficiently cultural view of the early years of development, and Bahktin's (1985) notions of addressivity and hidden dialogicality. From a CHAT perspective, words are the cultural artifacts through which the cognitive development-understanding of individuals and cultural groups can be accessed.

A CHAT perspective is concerned particularly with the role of cultural tools and signs (Wertsch, 1991). The social and developmental emphasis views speech as a cultural tool producing meaning rich linguistic signs. From this perspective, studying one's speech during problem solving is less centered on inferring processes through an analysis of information revealed through spoken words, and more concerned with looking at how speech both serves a social and developmental engagement in task-related activities and represents developmental changes across the life span (Smagorinsky, 1998, p. 4).

The CHAT approach assumes that a verbal protocol ought to be grounded in everyday life events, and assumes that mind emerges in the joint mediated activity of people. Toulmin also (1999) emphasizes the practical wisdom (or prudence) that is the focus of activity theory: "Language has a definite meaning only when it is related to a given constellation of practical activities" (p. 61). Mind, then, is co-constructed and distributed, and activity theory focuses on local, particular knowledge, what Tikhomirov (1999) calls *anti-algorithmic knowledge*. Individuals are active agents in their own development but do not act in settings entirely of their own making. CHAT rejects a simplistic cause-effect, stimulus-response approach in favor of one that emphasizes the emergent nature of mind in activity.

This social embeddedness is critical to the CHAT perspective, as it suggests careful attention be paid to the often limited generalizability of understandings about how people make meaning. For example, problem solving is a function of both how problems are defined in particular environments and how people have historically solved those problems with particular cultural goals in mind. Problem solving is thus a situated practice that is *not* generalizable across cultures, since cultural values, goals, practices, tools, and signs have historically developed to achieve different ends. Adopting a CHAT perspective then leads the evaluator to think more contextually, to consider the local environment (whether based on regionality, socioeconomic status, gender, and so on) in understanding the value of computer hardware and software (Nardi, 1996).

Unlike an IP perspective, the CHAT perspective does not attempt to neutralize the effects of the evaluator participant interaction—this is not contamination but a critical element for illuminating what things mean. Rather than presenting predetermined tasks or problems, CHAT designates task construal as the first step in meaning making; it reveals the participant's level of conceptual understanding and interpretations of signs, and is critical to developing an intersubjective relationship between evaluator and participant. So, for example, whereas an IP verbal protocol approach would have the evaluator physically behind the participant and minimally engaged, the CHAT verbal protocol approach would have the evaluator beside the participant in the role of an interlocutor aiming to facilitate the manifestation of a hidden dialogue about the what, why, and how of the computer—participant interaction.

Speech, therefore, does not reveal an internal process, but rather a process that reflects the cultural practices internalized through participation in speech-based interactions— interactions that in turn act on social contexts through more speech-based interactions (Toulmin, 1999). The analysis of verbal protocols does not therefore enable inferences about the individual mind, but rather should be seen as situated practice with antecedent cultural history.

CHAT, though a more useful theoretical underpinning for verbal protocol analysis, is not without its own challenges.

- History can only be partially reconstructed and thus cultural precedents for a protocol response are necessarily a sampling.
- The data from the verbal protocol is a narrative, likely to be long, and not easily summarized in simple ways.
- Evaluators are a significant part of the construction of meaning and therefore their cultural context matters greatly.

Case Example: Reading the Web (Continued)

Returning to the example of the Reading the Web Project, how has this project evolved? Although the authors concluded their summary of the early stages of the project by suggesting the need for further refinement of the task (that is, greater control of the context for data elicitation), some of the researchers suggested a different direction. This new direction was based on the following issues: (1) the WWW is a medium that has a variety of text forms and therefore requires a special type of reading comprehension, (2) the particular texts being read might be less important than prior knowledge and skills, and (3) authentic tasks are likely to yield a useful understanding, both in a theoretical and practical sense, of how people read the Web and how learning might be fostered in the use of this form of "text."

The second stage of the research has therefore moved into "real" educational settings, that is, school classrooms, where children are using the Internet for a variety of purposes. The methodology focuses more on observations of children doing "authentic" tasks (in this case, at least tasks contextualized in the school work and evidencing at least some degree of choice on the part of students). The verbal protocols focus on mutual interaction between evaluators and students about the how and why of Reading the Web. The data being collected are in many ways similar to the IP stage of the research (observations, verbal protocols, video screen recordings, and interviews). Most notable here, however, is that the use of verbal protocols from the IP perspective have been abandoned. Tasks are not set by the evaluators, nor are they uniform for all the participants. Verbal reports of participants still seek access to the short-term memory of participants, but not in isolation from the evaluator or the participants' reflections and associations with their prior experiences, knowledge, and skills. The shift suggests that participants can say what they are thinking, but also are able, in interaction with the evaluator, to say why they are thinking this, including revealing much about their personal history and the cultural capital they bring to the experience, as well as the impact of Reading the Web on other knowledge and skills. Reading the Web is therefore seen as a social act, one that is informed in an immediate and a conceptual way by the race, gender, class, ethnicity, and other characteristics of the reader.

Less well developed, but still an important aspect of the redirection of this project, is the exploration of the notion of Reading the Web as a culturally and socially embedded practice. In other words, not only are the experiences of individuals culturally, historically, and socially embedded, but so too is the overall practice of Reading the Web. These researchers have begun to explore the meaning of Reading the Web not just as a phenomenon that occurs as individuals sit before Internet-connected computers, but also as a social practice within schools, districts, and states. What happens in the individual—machine interaction is significantly informed by what happens in the policy and decision making arenas. This development suggests the limited nature of the verbal protocol as a means for making fully informed judgments of the value of any hardware or software intervention. The classroom data collection is therefore being enhanced by efforts to understand the perspectives of other stakeholders, such as school administrators, local and state policymakers, the local business community, parents, and taxpayers.

Lessons for Evaluating Software and Hardware

The evolution of this project that attempts to understand how people read the WWW, with an interest in understanding cognitively how this is done as well how such literacy might be fostered, provides a number of lessons for evaluating computer software and hardware.

- Verbal protocols can facilitate evaluations focusing on either process or outcomes. Much of the evaluation of computer technology has focused on outcomes, especially through the use of experimental designs, by look-ing for correlations between the computer use conditions and other condi-tions (such as student achievement in general). Formative studies have been more likely to examine the person-computer interactions, themselves. We would suggest that verbal protocols can serve both purposes. The case for this is more clearly made in the literature on formative evaluations, and so we focus mostly on advocating the use of this method in summative evalu-ations. The verbal protocol gets inside the interaction between the person and the computer, which is useful not only for development purposes but also for making decisions about adoption, curriculum development, and the effects of differential access to computers.

• It is important, perhaps critical, to use authentic applications when judging the value of software and hardware. Within the IP perspective, mak-ing the tasks invisible is considered important in order to get at "real" cog-nitive processing. CHAT, however, suggests there is no such thing as an invisible task. In other words, the task matters and trying to evaluate com-puter technologies through artificial tasks is no more defensible than other forms of unauthentic testing. We will learn much more about how com-puters are used and how we might enhance that use if the tasks are authen-tic. Tasks may be authentic in the sense they are part of the school culture or in the sense of being chosen by and thus especially relevant to individu-als involved in the evaluation.

• Evaluation should seek representations of complex technology uses mediated by many cultural, social factors. The first stage of the Reading the Web project concluded that each individual used unique strategies for completing the task. It seems unlikely that these strategies are indeed totally idiosyncratic and more likely that they represent culturally pat-terned ways of doing the task. The completion of any task, computer based or not, is probably complex. Data collection strategies that seek to disentangle this complexity (or at least not ignore it) will provide much greater insight about the values of technology. Nardi and O'Day (1999) suggest that it is important to ask questions to help us to describe the sit-uation, but we must also ask questions that "dig deeper," questions about visions, alternatives, consequences, obstacles, personal interests, and about what we ought to do.

• Evaluations of technology, like all evaluation, should exercise caution in making generalizations. Evaluators everywhere remember Cronbach's proclamation: "Generalizations decay." Cronbach (1982) was alluding mostly to the complexity of causality and our inability to fully comprehend all of the interrelated factors that account for things happening or not. In addition, activity theory suggests that generalizations are affected by issues such as gender, ethnicity, socioeconomic status, age, and so on, and that we ought to be very cautious in making grand generalizations about the how, why, and advisability of adopting and using computer software and hardware. Cron-bach's notion of external validity holds here more than ever—people appro-priately will make claims for themselves based on a synthesis of evaluation studies and their own contextual knowledge, not on the basis of definitive claims from one or even many evaluation studies.

• Verbal protocols alone are an inadequate basis for any evaluation. Activity theory suggests a certain approach to the use of verbal protocols, which from our case example seems to net greater understandings about the how, why, and "what if" of Reading the Web. However, no method in and of itself is sufficient to adequately evaluate anything. Interventions are multidimensional (whether they are meant to be or not), and the need for triangulation ought to be self-evident. Verbal protocols give a particularly useful view of the person-computer interaction, but there are many facets of technology that cannot be evaluated with this method alone. The Reading the Web project illustrates that the policy, decision-making context is as important for judging the value of computer adoptions in school, for example.

• The contexts of technology use are complex and social, and both methods and philosophical perspectives must take this into account. Nardi and O'Day (1999) suggest it is most important to look at "information ecologies," which they define as systems of people, practices, technologies, and values in a local environment. They further suggest having a responsible, informed engagement with technology in local settings where the spotlight is on human activities served by technology, not on the technology itself. A similar point is made by Newman (1997) in his explication of the construct of "functional learning environments." Computers are, he suggests, a significant part of a functional learning environment, although he accords the coordination of teachers' and students' points of view as more important in judging the value of a technology. The Reading the Web project has moved fruitfully in this direction by the inclusion of multiple perspectives beyond the computer-person interaction, a direction fully supported by activity theory.

Notes

1. Authors names are listed alphabetically; all contributed equally to this chapter.

2. The case example used here is derived from work currently being done by the Technology and Literate Thinking Group of the Center for English Learning and Achievement (CELA), supported under the Research and Development Center Program (Grant number R117G10015) as administered by the Office of Educational Research and Improvement, U. S. Department of Education. The findings and opinions expressed herein do not necessarily reflect the position or priorities of the sponsoring agency, CELA, or the Technology and Literate Thinking Group. One of the authors has been and continues to be involved in this project.

References

Bahktin, M. M. *Problems of Dostoevsky's Poetics*. Minneapolis: University of Minnesota Press, 1985.

Baker, E. L., Gearhart, M., and Herman, J. L. "Evaluating the Apple Classrooms of Tomorrow." In E. L. Baker and H. F. O'Neil Jr. (eds.), *Technology Assessment in Education and Training*. Hillsdale, N.J.: Erlbaum, 1994.

Baker, E. L., Niemi, D., and Herl, H. "Using Hypercard Technology to Measure Under-standing." In E. L. Baker and H. F. O'Neil Jr. (eds.), *Technology Assessment in Education and Training*. Hillsdale, N.J.: Erlbaum, 1994.

Blease, D. *Evaluating Educational Software*. Dover, N.H.: Croom Helm, 1986.

Bracewell, R. J., and Breuleux, A. "Substance and Romance in Analyzing Think-Aloud Protocols." In P. Smagorinsky (ed.), *Speaking About Writing: Reflections on Research Methodology*. Thousand Oaks, Calif.: Sage, 1994.

Cole, M. "Context, Modularity, and the Cultural Constitution of Development." In L. T. Winegar and Valsiner (eds.), *Children's Development Within Social Context, Volume 2: Research and Methodology*. Hillsdale, N.J.: Erlbaum, 1992.

Cole, M. *Cultural Psychology: A Once and Future Discipline*. Cambridge, Mass.: Harvard University Press, 1996.

Cole, M., Engeström, Y., and Vasquez, O. (eds.) *Mind, Culture, and Activity*. Cambridge: Cambridge University Press, 1997.

Cronbach, L. J. *Designing Evaluations of Educational and Social Programs*. San Francisco: Jossey-Bass, 1982.

Engström, Y. "Concepts of Activity Theory." In Y. Engeström, R. Miettinen, and R. L. Punamäki (eds.), *Perspectives on Activity Theory*. Cambridge: Cambridge University Press, 1999.

Ericsson, K. A., and Simon, H. A. "Verbal Reports as Data." *Psychological Review*, 1980, 87, 215–253.

Ericsson, K. A., and Simon, H. A. *Protocol Analysis: Verbal Reports as Data, Second Edition*. Cambridge, Mass.: MIT Press, 1993.

Flagg, B. N. *Formative Evaluation for Educational Technologies*. Hillsdale, N.J.: Erlbaum, 1990.

James, W. *The Principles of Psychology*. New York: Holt, 1890.

Johnston, J. "Research Methods for Evaluating the New Information Technologies." In J. Johnston (ed.), *Evaluating the New Information Technologies*, no. 23. San Francisco: Jossey-Bass, 1984.

Kulik, J. A. "Meta-Analytic Studies of Findings on Computer-Based Instruction." In E. L. Baker and H. F. O'Neil Jr. (eds.), *Technology Assessment in Education and Training*. Hillsdale, N.J.: Erlbaum, 1994.

Leont'ev, A. N. "On Approaches in Studies of Perception." In A. N. Leont'ev (ed.), *Perception and Activity*. Moscow: MGU Press, 1976.

Mitra, A., and Hullett, C. R. "Toward Evaluating Computer Aided Instruction: Attitudes, Demographics, Context." *Evaluation and Program Planning*, 1997, 20 (4), 379–391.

Nardi, B. A. (ed.) *Context and Consciousness: Activity Theory and Human-Computer Interaction*. Cambridge, Mass.: MIT Press, 1996.

Nardi, B. A., and O'Day, V. L. *Information Ecologies: Using Technology With Heart*. Cambridge, Mass.: MIT Press, 1999.

Newman, D. "Functional Environments for Microcomputers." In M. Cole, Y. Engeström, and O. Vasquez (eds.), *Mind, Culture, and Activity*. Cambridge: Cambridge University Press, 1997.

Pariset, M. "An Evaluation Instrument for Training Software." In A. McDougall and C. Dowling (eds.), *Computers in Education*. Amsterdam: Elsevier, 1990.

Pressley, M., and Afflerbach, P. *Verbal Protocols of Reading: The Nature of Constructively Responsive Reading*. Hillsdale, N.J.: Erlbaum, 1995.

Smagorinsky, P. "Thinking and Speech and Protocol Analysis." *Mind, Culture, and Activity*, 1998, 5 (3), 157–177.

Swan, K., Bowman, J., Holmes, A., Schweig, S., and Vargas, J. "Reading the Web: Making Sense on the Information Superhighway." *Journal of Educational Technology Systems*, 1998, 27 (2), 95–104.

Tickhomirov, O. K. "Theory of Activity and Information Technology. "In Y. Engeström, R. Miettinen, and R. L. Punamäki (eds.), *Perspectives on Activity Theory*. Cambridge: Cambridge University Press, 1999.

Tichener, E. B. "Prolegomena to Study of Introspection." *British Journal of Psychology,* 1920, *1,* 427–448.

Toulmin, S. "Knowledge as Shared Procedures." In Y. Engeström, R. Miettinen, and R. L. Punamäki (eds.), *Perspectives on Activity Theory.* Cambridge: Cambridge University Press, 1999.

Vygotsky, L. S. "Thinking and Speech." In R. W. Rieber and A. S. Carton (eds.). *The Collected Works of L. S. Vygotsky: Problems of General Psychology, Including the Volume Thinking and Speech (Cognition and Language).* New York: Plenum, 1987.

Watson, J. B. "Psychology as the Behaviorist Views It." *Psychological Review,* 1913, *20,* 158–177.

Watson, J. B. "Is Thinking Merely the Action of Language Mechanisms?" *British Journal of Psychology,* 1920, *1,* 87–104.

Wertsch, J. V. *Voices of the Mind: A Sociocultural Approach to Mediated Action.* Cambridge, Mass.: Harvard University Press, 1991.

SANDRA MATHISON is associate professor of education at the State University of New York in Albany, New York.

TRICIA R. MEYER is a doctoral candidate in education at the State University of New York in Albany, New York.

JUAN D. VARGAS is a doctoral candidate in education at the State University of New York in Albany, New York.

6

New technologies challenge conventional notions of research ethics, thus requiring evaluators to creatively address new kinds of threats to privacy, confidentiality, anonymity, and the disposition of data and to develop alternative notions of professional identity and responsibility.

Ethical Implications of Computer-Mediated Evaluation

Tammy L. Bennington

The evaluation literature is replete with discussions of how to fit methods to the theoretical and practical concerns of particular evaluation activities. This volume has attempted to initiate a comparable discussion of issues of the fit and compatibility of research technologies with pragmatic and theoretical concerns in evaluation inquiry. The latter issue is complicated in today's technologically textured world by ethical concerns regarding the potential, harmful consequences of using electronic technologies and the violation of fundamental principles of ethical research. Many types of unobtrusive, computer-mediated data collection practices potentially raise questions of surveillance, "dataveillance," privacy rights, informed consent, anonymity, and confidentiality. In addition, subtle ethical issues emerge when we take seriously the role of research tools in differentially revealing and concealing aspects of reality, the types of human interactions enabled or disabled by different tools, and how emergent technologies blur fundamental cultural distinctions between the private and public, individual and social, and information and commodity. Some of those currently involved in the computing ethics dialogue perceive the ethical concerns raised by emerging information and communication technologies as so profoundly challenging to traditional ethical frameworks that a new multidisciplinary effort is required to adequately articulate and deal with them (Rogerson and Bynum, 1996).

In addressing the ethical implications of the use of these technologies in evaluation practice, I share Schwandt's (1997, p. 26) position that "evaluators have a special obligation to foster discussion of public moral issues as they relate to the objects they evaluate, and they are also especially obliged to submit their own practice to normative scrutiny." Like Schwandt, I draw upon an understanding of ethics, the moral and the normative that extends beyond the narrow concerns and preoccupations of professional codes of ethics, to include the social-moral values and relationships that evaluation practices can serve to maintain or legitimate. Codes of ethics, even when reformulated as "guiding principles," tend to emphasize an ethics of rights and duties, excluding alternative ethical frameworks premised upon social justice, virtue, dignity, care, or trust. Too often they serve to maintain professional status and identity, rather than inspire serious and inclusive moral reflection. In the following discussion, I attempt to maintain an inclusive perspective premised upon a broadly defined, pragmatically oriented notion of ethics. My objective is not only to articulate and systematically conceptualize some fundamental moral concerns raised by computer-mediated inquiry, but also to encourage reflection on the types of communities and relationships we as evaluators desire. My purpose is to offer a critical, reflexive framework that raises awareness of technology-related ethical concerns and potentially facilitates informed ethical decision making regarding the use of diverse technologies in evaluation. This comprehensive approach to ethical issues comprises both a concern with rights, rules, and justice ("What should we do?") and concern with the quality and maintenance of relationships between evaluator and stakeholders, evaluators and public, and among evaluators themselves ("What sort of persons or community should we be?").

A Relational Ethic

The code of ethics, or "Guiding Principles for Evaluators" (GPfE), formulated by the American Evaluation Society lays out general guidelines intended both to inform evaluation professionals' practices and decision making and to establish the professional status of evaluation. In section C of the Preface, the GPfE notes that an intent of the Task Force was "to articulate a set of principles that should . . . inform evaluation clients and the general public about the principles they *can expect* [emphasis mine] to be upheld by professional evaluators" (American Evaluation Association, 1995). This statement provides a useful notion of ethics and guiding principles in that it turns our attention to the *expectations* that clients, and the public more widely, hold regarding evaluators' (*as* professionals) actions. The ethical import of actions can be understood to lie in the degree to which clients' expectations are met or are violated in their engagements with evaluators. These expectations derive from how we invoke and negotiate "professional" identity, responsibilities, obligations, degrees of agency, and motivations in our roles as evaluators. These expectations will vary, to a certain degree, with each evaluation project, with different objectives and with the different kinds of relationships established between the evaluator(s) and stakeholders.

But as recognized in the GfPE, in order to maintain and draw upon a collective "professional" identity, evaluators as a group must maintain a number of relatively shared social and moral commitments, particularly on sensitive ethical topics such as the prevention of harm, the disposition of data, technology use, and accountability. Negotiating shared commitments regarding computer-based technologies is particularly relevant to professional identity in light of the impact of computers on confidentiality, informed consent, and other ethical concerns enumerated in most professional codes of ethics. Simply from a pragmatic and utilitarian perspective, evaluator would be wise to acknowledge the ethical implications of increased dependence on computer-mediated data collection, and to articulate and encourage adherence to a set of guidelines regarding the collection, disposition, and uses of that data. Such actions can enhance the professional status of evaluation among a public wary of computer-assisted surveillance and increasingly skeptical of "professional" authority, a skepticism that has motivated the proliferation of professional ethics journals and codes of ethics since the early 1980s.

The "Non-Neutrality" of Technology and the Assumption of Ethical Responsibility

One can argue that technology and other cultural artifacts are not neutral; rather, they are "inherently ambiguous" (Ihde, 1990, p. 71) and entail affordances (properties that shape possible uses) and latent potentialities that are realized only in situated practice. Not only activity theory, as mentioned in Gay and Bennington's contribution to this volume, but also phenomenological approaches to technology emphasize the mediating and transformative roles that technology plays in human activities. The design, inherent characteristics, affordances, and social-cultural values inscribed in technologies all mediate human activities in complex but identifiable ways. For example, self-administered web-based surveys do not afford engagement between the evaluator and the respondent to negotiate meanings; e-mail interviewing can be fraught with problems if participants vary significantly in their styles of communication via the medium or in their perceptions of the medium; electronic tracking of computer users keystroke-by-keystroke can reveal patterns concealed by other data collection methods. Models such as activity theory are especially useful for explicating how this mediation works and thereby facilitating responsible moral decision making regarding the use of any technology. Viewing technology as neutral, in fact, can absolve those who design and implement technologies from responsibility for the moral implications of its use in practice (Coyne, 1995, p. 77). Ladd (1991, p. 666) refers to such a position as an "ethical cop-out."

In light of this non-neutrality, the ethical responsibility of the evaluator resides, in part, in anticipating the full range of consequences that could ensue from the use of a particular tool. The mediating effects of a technology emerge through its use in a particular social context and are shaped by participants' objectives and by characteristics of the encompassing community and use activity. Informed decision making therefore necessitates an imaginative process (Johnson, 1993) akin to scenario planning. The evaluator needs to identify the relevant features and uses of the technology, the purpose of the evaluation, the needs as well as expectations of the diverse stakeholders, and the social context of the evaluation. She then needs to lay out diverse cause-effect scenarios or narrative projections based on those identifications. This exercise can raise awareness of potential ethical issues that an evaluation activity might pose, and can provide an evaluator with an opportunity to prospectively articulate relevant moral frameworks and values that might inform decision making and resolution of the moral dilemmas that arise.

The previous chapters in this volume offer numerous computer-based and electronic tools for the collection and analysis of different forms of data in evaluation projects and for the reflexive meta-evaluation of the role of technology in evaluation activities—tracking devices, web-based surveys, video, and synchronous and asynchronous interactive communication spaces. The ethical concerns and dilemmas that technology use potentially raises can be loosely categorized in terms of privacy issues, social and individual control, the moral dimensions of "distanced" forms of engagement, and the revealing and concealing potentiality of technologies.

Privacy, Anonymity, and the Collapse of Public–Private Distinction

The ability to track the actions of computer users can provide rich, thickly textured descriptions and understandings of technology use, including how service recipients navigate electronically delivered services, how a particular computer application affects decision making or productivity, and how communication in an organization is affected by new technologies. Web surveys enable rapid and inexpensive data collection from particular populations and allow for randomization, reuse of previous answers, and intelligent interviewing techniques (Kottler, 1997). Digital video also provides new forms of data, analysis, and understanding. However, these tools simultaneously enable the surveillance and identification of individuals and groups, and thereby jeopardize privacy, confidentiality, and anonymity and provide information that can potentially be used to harm identified individuals or groups. Unless mediated by anonymous service providers or technologies, Web visits are logged, others can read one's e-mail, on-line chat can be logged, and participants' identities traced.

Dataveillance is a term that has been coined to refer to the use of information for the "monitoring of people not through their actions, but through data trails about them" (Clarke, 1997). Personal dataveillance of an individual can include integrating data stored in different locations in an organization, screening transactions, and front-end auditing of transactions by an organization or program (Clarke, 1991, p. 503). Dataveillance is facilitated by *data matching* (Shattuck, 1991), the matching of related computerized files or databases to identify possible illegal or suspicious activities on the part of individuals or to identify consumption or behavioral patterns for marketing purposes. In both cases, information collected for a particular purpose is used at a later time for very different purposes, thereby violating the expectations of those who initially provided the information as well as the expectations and obligations of those who collected it. Organizations, including businesses, government agencies, nonprofits, and health care providers are increasingly reliant upon publicly accessible data compiled from diverse sources for delivering customized services. The compilation of detailed information on individuals is facilitated and legitimated by a number of social-economic-technological developments, including globalization, the convergence of information systems, and increasingly facile translations among multimedia (Privacy International, n.d.). The pervasive use of electronic records and the dissemination of the information they contain among organizations, including health care and human and government services providers, pose significant threats to personal privacy. Considering the commodity status of information in today's world, evaluators must be especially attentive to their possible complicity in the exchange of sensitive information.

The moral issues posed by dataveillance and data matching are raised by many computer-mediated evaluation practices, namely, the absence of the "real" or embodied person from the "virtual" encounter (and hence their lack of awareness and control over the use of data), the potential, harmful uses of identifying data, the use of data for purposes other than those for which it was collected, the unanticipated co-optation of seemingly benign information for less benign purposes via data matching or data mining. Because of the potential threats to privacy, anonymity, and confidentiality posed by technologically mediated data collection, evaluators need to anticipate these threats and incorporate all stakeholders' concerns into the negotiation of project plans, particularly in light of the increasing privatization of evaluation activities. The disposition of primary data collected via these tools needs to be unambiguously resolved so as to maintain confidentiality, protect the anonymity of stakeholders when anonymity has been guaranteed, and minimize or eliminate the harm that such data could be used to perpetrate. These negotiations become critical as more and more data are collected and disseminated via the Internet (Johnson, 1996; Marson, 1997). In fact, in light of the commoditization of highly personal data such as mental health and human services records today, some professional organizations, such as the American Psychological Association, have begun to explicitly address computer technologies in their codes of ethics (Gelman, Pollack, and Weiner, 1999).

Negotiations regarding the use of data collected for evaluation purposes need to be held in good faith and with a certain degree of trust among evaluators and stakeholders. The evaluator needs to develop a degree of familiarity with the cultures, histories, and values of the evaluation sponsor(s) and other stakeholders in order to adequately assess whether they are likely to adhere to agreements regarding the disposition and use of data through which individuals can be identified. When such data remain in the possession of project sponsors, their possible harmful uses should be negotiated to protect vulnerable individuals or groups; for example, preventing employers from using tracking data collected to evaluate the usability of a computer system for purposes of performance evaluation, or preventing video data collected in the evaluation of training programs from being used to evaluate individual students (see Nardi and others, 1995, for an example of such data collection). Another relevant example would be the valuable marketing information created through evaluation activities such as the evaluation of a library's on-line catalog system, through which users' identities can potentially be tracked. How that information is stored and its potential sale should be directly addressed.

Such issues have become serious in today's information society in light of the ease and speed with which large quantities of information can be stored, retrieved, transmitted, and manipulated and because so many systems are not secure. These considerations highlight the extent to which ethical considerations entail the negotiation of relationships, not simply adherence to prescriptive and proscriptive guidelines. They expand professional ethics beyond concerns with the prevention of harm and protection of subjects (a negative ethics), to the at least minimalist articulation of the socially and morally "good" (a positive ethics).

Maintaining or guaranteeing the privacy of individual participants in a project can pose significant challenges when computer-mediated data are used. Clarke (1997) characterizes "privacy" as "the interest that individuals have in sustaining a 'personal space,' free from interference by other people and organizations." He uses this broad understanding of privacy to include not only the very narrow, and often nonexistent, legal right to privacy, but also related notions such as data protection and informational self-determination, which have acquired legal force in Europe. This expanded notion of privacy, which applies not only to persons but also to data about them, refers to freedom from unwarranted or unsolicited intrusion into personal spaces and can encompass both legal and socially accepted privacy "rights" regarding information privacy, bodily privacy, privacy of communications, and territorial privacy (Privacy International, n.d.). This understanding of privacy, as Ladd (1991) notes, challenges the received definition of the term, which is concerned with the violations of physical boundaries and spaces. It might behoove evaluators, if as a profession they wish to maintain public trust, to adopt this expanded notion of privacy in light of public suspicion of computer-generated and mediated data and fears of privacy violation (Cranor, Reagle, and Ackerman, 1999; Privacy International, n.d.). Assuming a proactive, committed stance on information privacy and the use of computer-mediated data collection becomes more imperative considering the widespread violation of privacy laws by corporations and the increasing prominence of information privacy as an international human rights issue.

Tracking or recording computer-mediated activities such as e-mail correspondence, website navigation, on-line chat and on-line surveys, and the use of databases such as electronic library systems all create potentially sensitive data that can violate expectations of privacy. They can also violate confidentiality, which differs from privacy in that it refers to "the duty of individuals who come into possession of information about others" (Clarke, 1997). The expectations and obligations at play in issues of confidentiality derive from the relationships of trust established between evaluator and stakeholders, sponsors and evaluator, and among various stakeholders. Confidentiality, implied or formally guaranteed (and it is usually expected of professionals *qua* professionals), is often necessary for eliciting or accessing sensitive or personal information. Confidentiality entails concomitant responsibilities for assuring the anonymity of data, that is, dissociating data from any information that can be used to identify its source in an individual. Cranor, Reagle, and Ackerman (1999) note Web users' hesitancy to furnish information over the Internet unless they are provided with information regarding the purpose of its collection, its future use, and whether they could be identified by the information provided. Researchers who rely upon web-based elicitation of information assume responsibility for protecting subjects and can minimize respondents' concerns by using encryption for the transmission of data, providing information on or access to anonymous remailers (such as Potato, Privtool, or Mixmaster) to respondents, and ensuring the security of Web-based chat spaces, sometimes used for virtual group interviews. They can further reassure respondents by clearly indicating the level of security for any particular computer-mediated activity.

These expectations of anonymity, confidentiality, privacy, and the appropriate use of information need to be taken seriously in that their fulfillment provides the grounds of trust necessary for conducting effective evaluation. The significance and nature of that trust in the design and execution of evaluation activities, however, varies with the differing theoretical and political perspectives of evaluators and stakeholders. As noted above, the moral dimensions of human relationships can be understood as deriving from a mutual recognition of expectations. It is when the expectations parties have of one another are unfulfilled that the moral and ethical questions of intent, motivation, and accountability arise. Therefore, it is in the interest of evaluators as a group to collectively and consistently address ethical issues such as privacy in a manner that fosters public trust in the profession of evaluation, in part through clearly articulating roles, objectives, methods, and expectations throughout the evaluation process.

When it comes to anonymity, privacy, and the collection of detailed information on individuals via computer-based technologies, the evaluator often has to resolve oppositions such as the privacy rights of the individual versus employers' or others' need for information; full disclosure and informed consent versus the evaluator's need to elicit reliable and valid information; and under what conditions and for what purposes should the collected data be shared. These issues and deliberations are not unique to technologically mediated data collection, but the consequences of the decisions can have more serious ramifications for evaluation participants in today's electronically interconnected world and information-based economy.

Furthermore, the unique features of electronic communication and information systems are transforming distinctions between the private and public realms, upon which our society's legal and organizational structures are premised and around which expectations are formed. This blurring, legal and social, is particularly evident in debates over the status of the Internet (Is it a public or private forum?) and the status of information solicited and collected through it. Legally, it has not been defined as public and hence individuals' actions via the Internet can be tracked and identified according to the policies and interests of service providers. But again, many Internet users engage in diverse activities with assumptions and expectations of privacy. Likewise, groupware applications and intranets in workplaces are not public fora with associated rights, though many employees might use intranet services with expectations of privacy and no thought as to how information derived from that use might be employed for purposes of evaluation, research, or surveillance. Currently in the United States, legally and socially these issues come down in the last instance to who has *access* and *control* over the various types of information—content, tracking, interactional—produced through the diverse uses of these technologies. However, the confusion and ambiguity regarding privacy attests to the coevolution of technology and the socio-legal understandings and regulations of its use (Stewart and Williams, 1998). Evaluators as professionals can help shape this coevolution and enhance their collective credibility through actively addressing these issues in ways that merit public trust, as social workers have begun to do (Phillips and Berman, 1995; Gelman, Pollack, and Weiner, 1999).

Individual, Collective, or Social Control Issues

"Control" is a pervasive metaphor throughout the use of computer-based technologies. As Kling (1991, p. 421) notes, "different ways of organizing control over computing resources . . . have an associated politics." Computing resources include the information collected and produced via computer applications. As noted in the above section, a critical concern in evaluation is negotiating and clarifying the conditions under which information will be collected and how it will be used and stored, which further depends, in our increasingly commoditized society, on who is perceived as *owning* it. Ownership and possession entail the ability, even the right, to control. Individuals possess only partial ownership, and hence control, of financial records collected on them by banks or credit unions (Kling, 1991). An organization owns the information it collects on individual employee performance and activities, including video data, performance appraisals, and computer-tracking information. These ownership issues warrant explicit discussion when an evaluation inquiry relies upon an intranet or an organization's collaborative groupware system as sources of data or as means of involving stakeholder participation in the inquiry. With the commoditization of information, ownership entails the right to sell and purchase information independently of the purposes, conditions, or contexts in which the information was initially compiled or created. However, legislation recently proposed in the California state senate is beginning to challenge this by prohibiting "the collection, use, and disclosure of any type of personally identifiable information without the consent of the record subject" (Privacy Forum, 1999).

Intimately related to the issue of individual control are the practices of full disclosure and informed consent. Of concern in conducting web-based evaluation, whether observing conduct in cyberspace or soliciting feedback via web-based surveys, is that those who participate in such data collection be fully informed of the purposes of the research and its attendant risks and benefits, and have the opportunity to pose questions and obtain clarification on the purpose and conduct of the project if they request it. Full disclosure includes informing participants of the degree of security and anonymity in, for example, Web-based exchanges. Moreover, informed consent entails ascertaining that participants comprehend the information provided to them. Assessing the degree of comprehension of a "virtual" participant in a web-based environment is difficult to accomplish and may require more attention to clarity and detail in the written materials that solicit participation. Stakeholders' effective control over the dissemination and use of information collected on them and collected directly from them depends on fully informed consent and the maintenance of contact over time to ensure that consent is obtained regarding future uses of that information.

Again, it is important that evaluators confront their own political and moral commitments and assumptions and articulate them in order to perceive the larger picture in which an evaluation is situated and in which technology-related ethical concerns emerge. Evaluators committed to participatory, empowerment, or other collaborative approaches to evaluation usually address diverse control-related issues explicitly because the redistribution of power or the transformation of power relations is an objective of the evaluation. However, in many other approaches, presuppositions and attitudes regarding power and control are often left implicit. Critical reflection is enlightening whether one wishes to maintain a value-neutral stance or committed value stance in the evaluation activity itself. Questions an evaluator can ask herself to stimulate reflection and provoke awareness include, "What are my views regarding the degree of access and control individuals should have over information collected on them?" "What are my views regarding information as commodity?" "Do I tend to perceive technology as a social good?" "What are my assumptions regarding the relationship between the individual and the state or the corporation?" "What are the implications of evaluators' using data collected by employers for performance monitoring?" The answers to such questions orient one's predispositions toward ethical dilemmas, particularly the value and import of privacy and control, posed by the use of information technologies. One needs to reflect on how one's values regarding rights, ownership, social justice, and the individual/social relationship influence one's actions and how they might differ from the values of other stakeholders. One can then incorporate those reflections into a more complex, multidimensional model of privacy that acknowledges the interests, rights, and needs of multiple stakeholders, including the evaluators (Stone and Stone-Romero, 1998). The profession of evaluation needs collectively to ask these questions and formally articulate collective positions in an era of increasing computer-mediated surveillance (Privacy International, n.d.).

Ethical Implications of Distanced Engagement

The use of any particular technology raises ethical concerns not only in regards to the conditions and consequences of its use, but also in regards to the displacement or replacement of other technologies. An evaluator has multiple options in choosing tools and methods for data collection and analysis. This selection process entails assessing and comparing the advantages and disadvantages of the various options and hence is fraught with ethical implications. The selection of data collection tools necessitates weighing their advantages *in relation to* alternative tools that could be or formerly were used to collect similar data and in terms of the types of human interactions they enable.

Many emergent technologies enable the collection of data from a physical or temporal distance, that is, without face-to-face encounters. For example, interviewing via teleconferencing or facilitating group dialogue via an on-line, text-based discussion space, even photography (Gold, 1989), raises concerns about the quality of interpersonal and group interaction. This quality can be an important valuative criterion in multiple ethical frameworks, but is particularly relevant if one approaches moral decision making from an ethics-of-care (Gilligan, 1982; Oliner and Oliner, 1995), virtue (MacIntyre, 1981; Nussbaum, 1986), sensitivity (Gold, 1989), or attunement perspective (Marx, 1992). From such perspectives, the type and quality of relationships, including research relationships, are fundamental ethical concerns, as they are from feminist or empowerment evaluation perspectives. Hence, if one approaches the selection process from one of these latter approaches, one might make technology-related decisions that are very different from those of a person whose central ethical concern is fairness based on the equality or similarity of treatment. Distanced interaction with others—for example, through an electronic communication space limited to asynchronous interaction—eliminates the immediate bodily and facial cues that can foster, though not ensure, a sense of immediacy, presence, and intimacy as well as empathy and shared understanding (Kiesler, Siegel, and McGuire, 1991). Such technologically mediated communication tools are informed by a model of communication as the transfer of information from one disembodied mind to another. If the purpose of an interaction is simply to convey information, such a tool might be appropriate; but if the purpose is to establish rapport and trust in order to elicit insights into sensitive matters, a face-to-face, embodied engagement might be preferable. Moreover, some respondents may feel more comfortable with or respond more positively to face-to-face engagement (Beebe and others, 1997). Riedel and others (1998) note how computer anxiety can differentially affect persons' access to and use of electronic networks, thereby exacerbating inequalities within a community. Alemagno, Frank, Mosavel, and Butts (1998) discuss the advantages and disadvantages of using an interactive voice response system to screen adolescents for health risks. Physicians expressed concern that the impersonal system detracted from the quality of the physician-patient relationship. However, computer-mediated communication can minimize certain forms of social control and hierarchy in communicative interactions, thus enabling more egalitarian interactions. Achieving intimacy via more distanced forms of interaction is not impossible, but requires forethought in the design and facilitation of the interaction. A further moral implication of the disembodied nature of computer-mediated communication is contingent upon one's rationale for using the media. Desiring to "transcend" the "limitations" of the body, including its local and temporal situatedness, is an often heard rationale and justification for using distanced forms of evaluation. Such rhetoric, however, entails an implicit devaluation of embodied experience and situatedness. A rhetoric and worldview that maintains the value of transcending the body is especially problematic for those who see the body or the face as fundamentally constitutive of moral and social perception, and for those who rely on experiential methodologies or view the embodied evaluator as herself a research tool.

Another concern in distanced engagement is assessing the credibility of participants. Pseudonymity—that is, engaging in on-line interactions under alternative and often ambiguous identities—plays a not insignificant role in virtual interactions. Attempting to understand or evaluate virtual communities or activities, or to investigate actual communities and activities *through* distanced means, raises issues regarding the "true" identity, traits, and backgrounds of participants-respondents. Ambiguous identity further challenges the authenticity and contractual force of informed consent agreements.

The ethical implications of interaction at a distance are contingent then upon the particular circumstances of the evaluation as well as the ethical values and expectations of the evaluator(s) and of the community in which it is conducted. Practical considerations often constrain possibilities; fewer options exist, for example, when a geographically dispersed group is the focus of interest or when distanced engagement is preferable to no engagement. More options and choices are possible when more "intimate" tools, such as face-to-face interviews or synchronous rather than asynchronous computer-mediated communications, are feasible. The numerous distancing effects of tools and methods can be considered in terms of their ethical implications; for example, the decontextualization and dissociation of the lived experiences of persons from abstracted forms of data, such as survey responses or electronic archives; the possible reduction of evaluation participants to textual data when face-to-face engagement has not been feasible; the potential objectification of persons and interactions via visual representations; or, in a positive vein, the enhancement of interaction through the reduction of overt status indicators. It is this dissociation, or the creation of a "digital persona," that can facilitate and even justify—rationally, emotionally, and technically—dataveillance practices (Clarke, 1997) or the aggressive intrusiveness of some e-mail surveying noted by Sheehan and Hoy (1999).

A final ethical as well as methodological consideration is the way in which emergent technologies such as teleconferencing or online group interviewing mediate and potentially transform human relationships and activities. Does a particular communication tool, such as asynchronous web-based group interviewing, facilitate greater participation on the part of some participants than a traditional focus group? Or does the tool give greater import to the initial contributors, who then inordinately influence topic selection throughout the exchange? Such interactional features shape the quality of the experience, the quality of the relationships established during the course of the evaluation, as well as the information derived from it. We need to continually reflect on how technologies shape the realities, persons, objects, and activities we perceive *through* them.

Technologies such as video-conferencing, synchronous and asynchronous communication spaces, and web-based surveys mediate the experiences of all research participants, including evaluators. Reflecting on the ethical implications of that mediation is warranted by the moral nature of human interactions and by the possible epistemological consequences of those interactions in evaluation and research settings. Mediation may significantly impact on degrees of intimacy and immediacy and sense of presence (Lombard and Ditton, 1997). If intimacy and the rapport and trust it fosters are deemed consequential for eliciting sensitive information, evaluators can learn skills and techniques for enhancing the sense of presence and intimacy in the use of different technologies. Similarly, the skills required for individual and group interviewing from a distance differ from those in face-to-face interactions. Gaiser (1997) discusses the numerous challenges of facilitating meaningful on-line focus group interactions, including being flexible in an on-line setting, moderating controversy, providing space-time for equitable participation, and enhancing participants' comfort levels with the medium. And with emerging interactive technologies, even such tools as Web surveys can readily be designed to include interactive elements that facilitate a sense of presence and comfort on the part of both evaluators and those surveyed.

Technology as Revealing and Concealing Dimensions of Reality: Advocating "Mixed Technology" Evaluation

If technologies can be understood as means of revealing some aspects of reality and concealing others, as in Heideggerian-inspired frameworks (Coyne, 1995), a further ethical concern becomes the moral implications of how and whether those revealing-concealing potentialities are realized. For example, tracking the detailed navigational movements of a user of a computer-delivered program or educational experience can reveal patterns of behavior and decision making that are not within the conscious awareness of the user and that would not have been revealed through an interview or survey or by observation. Data matching, as noted above, reveals relationships among data with no apparent connections. The revealing-concealing metaphor is useful for conceptualizing the social, political, and ethical implications of any technology and for helping stakeholders reflect on what a particular technology conceals or deflects attention from in any evaluation activity, although the metaphor simultaneously obscures the constructionist aspects of knowledge. Of moral, epistemological, and ontological concern is not only what is revealed, but also the implications of how those revelations are represented (Shum, 1998).

Revelations can be seen as *represented* or, depending on one's epistemological and ontological assumptions, *constructed* or *mediated* through different technologies. When tracking data are collected on a user's navigation of a website, how does the representation of the tracks relate to the actual embodied activities of the user? Such representations simultaneously can reduce, amplify, or occlude dimensions of the actions or process represented. If a software application creates conceptual maps from text-based group interactions (see Trochim, n.d.), what is the relationship between those maps and the situated interactions? To what extent do representations gloss ambiguity, situatedness, context, and temporal relations? What do they conceal, neglect, or omit? These consideration are particularly significant in the use of computer technologies, because the design of those technologies and their capacity for revelation and representation are constructed from formalized digital representations of knowledge and from computational models (Shum, 1998). Shum (1998, p. 76) poses another pertinent question: "Does analysis of such representations make idealized assumptions which do not hold in the real world embodiments of the knowledge/expertise being modeled?" Researchers should remember that such representations are often second- or third-order abstractions from the object of study. Moreover, they can entail various degrees of reification or objectification of the phenomena represented.

As noted in Bennington, Gay, and Jones in this volume, visual representations and image technologies more generally tend to emphasize what is revealed at the expense of what is concealed (Ihde, 1993, p. 44). Because of culturally prescribed ways of reading and accepting visual images, we are too often naive in our perceptions of them. We ignore the effects of framing, transformation of context, temporal freezing, and relative isomorphism between an image and what it represents (Ihde, 1993, p. 47). However, as the use of multimedia becomes more prevalent in the construction and dissemination of results, these effects will be transformed; movement and temporality, at least, will become readily accessible presentational resources. Multimedia literacy, likewise, will become a more widespread skill, and it is hoped that those who consume images and multimedia texts will consume them with a more critical and perceptive understanding of their construction.

If we draw upon the reveal-conceal metaphor, we might propose a technological pluralism that corresponds to methodological pluralism (Greene and Caracelli, 1997), that is, the use of multiple tools for data collection and analysis that can reveal multiple valid understandings of a phenomenon. Multiple technologies can then be selected to enable a more comprehensive understanding of a program and to meet multiple objectives; that is, a pragmatic mixed-technology approach can be designed relying on a rationale comparable to that informing mixed-method evaluation. Such an approach is compatible with activity theory and fosters an attentiveness to the activities, social relationships, and learning mediated by the technology rather than to the technology itself as neutral tool.

One can argue that the use of multiple technologies, like the use of multiple methods, to collect, manage, and analyze data can reveal more complex, more nuanced, and richer understanding of the phenomenon of interest; the selection and use of those tools have moral implications that derive from this capacity to reveal or conceal reality. Not only does the selection of a tool have ethical significance in that it entails decisions regarding what will be "seen," so does the decision not to use a tool, in the sense that one is electing not to see dimensions of reality revealed by that tool. The example cited above of the evaluation of an interactive voice-response technology used to screen adolescents entailed determining the value of seeing adolescent's facial and embodied expression, which the technology concealed (Alemagno, Frank, Mosavel, and Butts, 1998). One assumes responsibility for not only the harms and benefits of the tools one uses, but for the unrealized benefits of those one does not use. As with anticipating other ethical dilemmas associated with technology use, the selection process can be facilitated through imaginative scenario planning that takes into consideration the different revelations of various technologies and the consequences of those revelations for understanding.

Conclusion

Donna Haraway, in her work on the social-moral implications of biotechnologies and informational technologies, asserts that "[k]nowledge-making technologies . . . must be made relentlessly visible and open to critical intervention" (1997, p. 36). From an activity theory perspective, the necessity of this "making visible and vulnerable" is a consequence of the mediating function of tools in human activities and relationships. The responsibility for making visible lies to a significant extent with those who select and implement technologies, including evaluators and researchers who use them for data collection, management, and analysis. Making visible the ethical implications of computer-based and other electronic tools for conducting evaluations entails several reflective processes:

- Reflecting on and articulating stakeholders', including evaluators', implicit and explicit ethical assumptions and frameworks that are relevant to the negotiation of roles and expectations for the evaluation activity
- Reflecting on and articulating all stakeholders' relevant implicit and explicit assumptions regarding technology and its uses
- Anticipating the social and ethical consequences, for the community and for the relationships among stakeholders and evaluators, of the mediating and transformative implications of the use of any technology
- Incorporating insights derived from the above reflections into participatory negotiations of evaluation contracts
- Fully disclosing the intentions and rationale(s) informing the use of technologies and the associated risks and benefits
- Assuming responsibility (of differing degrees, individual and collective) for the consequences that ensue from the use and the nonuse of technologies in evaluation

Through reflective practice we can identify, possibly anticipate, and preemptively address the social and ethical implications of our use of technology. We can, at least, prevent the tools we use from becoming transparent and thereby inaccessible to critical evaluation. As noted above, tools are not neutral but shape the social contexts within which they are used in identifiable ways. They mediate and can fundamentally transform communities (including relationships, social conventions and norms, and practices), the various agents participating in the activity, and the objectives of the activity—here, evaluation. Their selection needs to become an integral part of the design and negotiation of evaluation projects and subject to the same theoretical and epistemological scrutiny as the selection and integration of methods. The use of electronic and computer technologies are implicative for privacy, anonymity, confidentiality, subject autonomy, and the quality of relationships and interactions in evaluation activities.

Technologies further frame and are framed by the epistemological and ontological presuppositions of those who use them, and thereby play a constitutive role in processes of knowledge construction and representation. Evaluators have a responsibility, as part of the professional covenant, to raise awareness of and proactively address the ethical concerns posed by their selection and use.

References

Alemagno, S., Frank, S., Mosavel, J., and Butts, J. "Screening Adolescents for Health Risks Using Interactive Voice Response Technology: An Evaluation." *Computers in Human Services,* 1998, *15* (4), 27–37.

American Evaluation Association, Task Force on Guiding Principles of Evaluators. "Guiding Principles for Evaluators." In W. R. Shadish, D. L. Newman, M. A. Scheirer, and C. Wye (eds.), *Guiding Principles for Evaluators.* New Directions for Program Evaluation, no. 66. San Francisco: Jossey-Bass, 1995.

Beebe, T. J., Mika, T., Harrison, P. A., Anderson, R. E., and Fulkerson, J. A. "Computerized School Surveys: Design and Development Issues." *Social Science Computer Review,* 1997, *15* (20), 159–169.

Clarke, R. "Information Technology and Dataveillance." In C. Dunlop and R. Kling (eds.), *Computerization and Controversy: Value Conflicts and Social Choices.* Boston: Academic Press, 1991.

Clarke, R. "Privacy and Dataveillance, and Organisational Strategy." Xamax Consultancy Pty. Ltd, 1997. [http://www.anu.edu.au/people/Roger.Clarke/DV/PStrat.html].

Coyne, R. *Designing Information Technology in the Postmodern Age: From Method to Metaphor.* Cambridge, Mass., and London: MIT Press, 1995.

Cranor, L. F., Reagle, J., and Ackerman, M. S. "Beyond Concern: Understanding Net Users' Attitudes about Online Privacy." *AT&T Labs-Research Technical Report* TR99.4.3, 1999. [http://www.research.att.com/library/trs/TRs/99/99.4/99.4/].

Gaiser, T. J. "Conducting On-Line Focus Groups: A Methodological Discussion." *Social Science Computer Review,* 1997, *15* (2), 135–144.

Gelman, S. R., Pollack, D., and Weiner, A. "Confidentiality of Social Work Records in the Computer Age." *Social Work,* 1999, *44* (3), 243–252.

Gilligan, C. *In a Different Voice: Psychological Theory and Women's Development.* Cambridge, Mass.: Harvard University Press, 1982.

Gold, S. J. "Ethical Issues in Visual Fieldwork." In G. Blank, J. L. McCartney, and E.Brent (eds.), *New Technology in Sociology: Practical Applications in Research and Work.* New Brunswick and London: Transaction Publishers, 1989.

Greene, J. C., and Caracelli, V. J. "Defining and Describing the Paradigm Issue in Mixed-Method Evaluation." In J. C. Greene and V. J. Caracelli (eds.), *Advances in Mixed-Method Evaluation: The Challenges and Benefits of Integrating Diverse Paradigms.* New Directions for Evaluation, no. 74. San Francisco: Jossey-Bass, 1997.

Haraway, D. J. *Modest_Witness@Second_Millenium.FemaleMan©_Meets_OncoMouse™: Feminism and Technoscience.* New York and London: Routledge, 1997.

Ihde, D. *Technology and the Lifeworld: From Garden to Earth.* Bloomington and Indianapolis: Indiana University Press, 1990.

Ihde, D. *Postphenomenology: Essays in the Postmodern Context.* Evanston, Ill.: Northwest University Press, 1993.

Johnson, M. *Moral Imagination: Implications of Cognitive Science for Ethics.* Chicago and London: University of Chicago Press, 1993.

Johnson, P. L. "Evaluation of U.S. Public Health Service Programs: Organization and Management." *Evaluation and the Health Professions,* 1996, *19* (3), 311–324.

Kiesler, S., Siegel, J., McGuire, T. W. "Social Psychological Aspects of Computer-Mediated Communication." In C. Dunlap and R. Kling (eds.), *Computerization and Controversy: Value Conflicts and Social Choices.* Boston: Academic Press, 1991.

Kling, R. "Value Conflicts in the Design and Organization of EFT Systems." In C. Dunlop and R. Kling (eds.), *Computerization and Controversy: Value Conflicts and Social Choices.* Boston: Academic Press, 1991.

Kottler, R. E. "Exploiting the Research Potential of the World Wide Web." Presentation given at Research 97, London, October 1997. [http://www.spss.nl/spssmr/web_bureau/knowledge/r97a.htm].

Ladd, J. "Computers and Moral Responsibility: A Framework for an Ethical Analysis." In C. Dunlop and R. Kling (eds.), *Computerization and Controversy: Value Conflicts and Social Choice.* Boston: Academic Press, 1991.

Lombard, M., and Ditton, T. "At the Heart of It All: The Concept of Presence." *Journal of Computer Mediated Communication,* 1997, *3* (2). [http://www.ascusc.org/jcmc/vol3/issue2/lombard.html].

MacIntyre, A. C. *After Virtue: A Study in Moral Theory.* Notre Dame: University of Notre Dame Press, 1981.

Marson, S. M. "A Selective History of Internet Technology and Social Work." *Computers in Human Services,* 1997, *14* (2), 35-49.

Marx, W. *Towards a Phenomenological Ethics: Ethos and the Life-World.* Albany: State University of New York Press, 1992.

Nardi, B. A., Schwarz, H., Kuchinsky, A., Leichner, R., Whittaker, S., and Sclabassi, R. "Video-as-Data: Turning Away from Talking Heads." In S. J. Emmott (ed.), *Information Superhighways: Multimedia Users and Futures.* London: Academic Press, 1995.

Nussbaum, M. C. *The Fragility of Goodness: Luck and Ethics in Greek Tragedy and Philosophy.* Cambridge and New York: Cambridge University Press, 1986.

Oliner, P. M., and Oliner, S. P. *Toward a* Caring *Society: Ideas into Action.* Westport, Conn., and London: Praeger, 1995.

Phillips, D., and Berman, Y. *Human Services in the Age of New Technology: Harmonising Social Work and Computerisation.* Aldershot: Avebury, 1995.

Privacy Forum. "CA Bill Would Restrict Use of Personal Information." Privacy Forum Archive Document (priv.08.05), 1999. [http://www.vortex.com/privacy/priv.08.05].

Privacy International. "Privacy and Human Rights: An International Survey of Privacy Laws and Practice." [http://www.gilc.org/privacy/survey/intro.html]. (n.d.).

Reidel, E., Dresel, L., Wagoner, M. J., Sullivan, J. L., and Borgida, E. "Electronic Communities: Assessing Equality of Access in a Rural Minnesota Community." *Social Science Computer Review,* 1998, *16* (4), 370–390.

Rogerson, S., and Bynum, T. W. "Information Ethics: The Second Generation." 1996. [http://www.ccsr.cms.dmu.ac.uk/resources/general/discipline/ie_sec_gen.html].

Schwandt, T. A. "The Landscape of Values in Evaluation: Charted Terrain and Unexplored Territory." In D. J. Rog and D. Fournier (eds.), *Progress and Future Directions in Evaluation: Perspectives on Theory, Practice, and Methods.* New Directions for Evaluation, no. 76, 25–39. San Francisco: Jossey-Bass, 1997.

Shattuck, J. "Computer Matching Is a Serious Threat to Individual Rights." In C. Dunlop and R. Kling (eds.), *Computerization and Controversy: Value Conflicts and Social Choices.* Boston: Academic Press, 1991.

Sheehan, K. B., and Hoy, M. G. "Using E-Mail to Survey Internet Users in the United States: Methodology and Assessment." *Journal of Computer-Mediated Communication,* 1999, *4* (3) [http://www. ascusc.org/jcmc/vol4/issue3/sheehan.html]

Shum, S. B. "Negotiating the Construction of Organisational Memories." In U. M. Borghoff and R. Pareschi (eds.), *Information Technology for Knowledge Management.* Berlin: Springer, 1998.

Stewart, J., and Williams, R. "The Coevolution of Society and Mutimedia Technology: Issues in Predicting the Future Innovation and Use of a Ubiquitous Technology." *Social Science Computer Review,* 1998, *16* (3), 268–282.

Stone, D. L., and Stone-Romero, E. F. "A Multiple Stakeholder Model of Privacy in Organizations." In M. Schminke (ed.), *Managerial Ethics: Moral Management of People and Process.* Mahwah, N.J.: Erlbaum, 1998.

Trochim, W. M. K. "An Introduction to Concept Mapping for Planning and Evaluation." [http://trochim.human.cornell.edu/research/epp1/epp1.htm]. n.d.

TAMMY L. BENNINGTON is research associate in the Human-Computer Interaction Group at Cornell University and adjunct professor in the Program on Social and Organizational Learning at George Mason University.

INDEX

Activities: decontextualization from, 10–11; defining, 5; distanced evaluation and, 13–14, 98; evaluation as, 6; function of, 4–5; mediated by technical tools, 7

Activity theory approach: basis of, 79; function of technology in, 4–7; model of, 5; object-orientedness in, 6; recommendations of, 17–18; on technologically mediated evaluation, 8–11, 13–14, 61, 99; on verbal protocols, 84

Advertising Research Foundation, 40

Afflerbach, P., 74

Agent usage, 52–53

Alemagno, S., 97

American Psychological Association, 91

Anonymity issues, 90–94, *See also* Privacy issues

Anti-algorithmic knowledge, 80

Aristotle, 74

Art Museum Education Image Consortium (AMICO), 46

Asynchronous data collection, 49

Asynchronous evaluations, 56–57

Asynchronous list server discussions, 28–29

Atkinson, P., 9, 10

Audio data evaluation, 11–13, *See also* Video data

Audio, visual, and mixed media focus groups, 29–30

Audio-visual Internet interviews, 27

Automated evaluation services, 53

Bahktin, M. M., 80

Bennington, T. L., 3, 12, 15, 21, 59, 69, 72, 87, 89, 99, 103

Bruzzone, D., 40

Bryson, P., 12

Butts, J., 97

Caracelli, V. J., 60, 70

CATI (Computer Aided Telephone Interviewing), 25

CEVA, 61–62

CGI (Common Gateway Interface), 24–25, 26, 41

CHAT (cultural-historical activity theory), 74; compared to IP theory, 77; to evaluate software/hardware, 83; on verbal protocols, 79–81, 83

Clarke, R., 92

Coding, 9–10

Coffey, A., 9, 10

Cognition, 80

Collaboration: applications of technical tools in, 15–16; supported by use of video data, 67–68

Common Gateway Interface (CGI), 24–25, 26, 41

Communication applications, 15–16

Computer Aided Telephone Interviewing (CATI), 25

Computer-mediated evaluation: ethical implications of distanced, 96–98; ethical responsibility/non-neutrality of technology and, 89–90; GPfE (Guiding Principles for Evaluators) and, 88–89; privacy/anonymity issues of, 90–94; pseudonymity and, 97; social control of information and, 94–96, *See also* Evaluation

Concept mapping, 55

Constellations, 62–63

Contextual user feedback, 53–55

Cook, T. D., 8, 18

Cookies, 51–52

Cooperation rates: definitions of, 34; factors affecting, 34–35, 37–39; from Web surveys, 36

Cornell University, 4

Cronbach, L. J., 83

CueVideo, 63

Cultural tools/signs, 80–81

Cultural-historical activity theory (CHAT). *See* CHAT (cultural-historical activity theory)

Data matching, 91

Dataveillance, 90–94, 98, *See also* Privacy issues

Demographically defined population, 33

Digital video: analysis/integration of, 61–63; fluid and malleable nature of,

Vargas, J. D., 4, 73, 86

Verbal protocols: activity theory approach to, 84; CHAT on, 79–81, 83; described, 74; historical context of, 74–75; information processing theory and, 75–77, 83; Reading the Web project case study on, 77–79, 81–82, 84

"Verbal report", 76

Video data: analysis and integration of digital, 61–63; collaboration supported by use of, 67–68; convergence of multiple forms in, 66; evaluation use of, 11–13; limitations in evaluation, 68–70, *See also* Multimedia records

VideoVISTA, 63

Visual Basic, 25

Vygotsky, L. S., 4, 79–80

Watson, J. B., 75

Watt, J. H., 23, 43

Web Common Gateway Interface (CGI) programs, 24–25, 26, 41

Web focus groups, 27–29

Web page annotators, 54–55

Web surveys: bursty nature of, 39; cooperation rates from, 36; selecting to use, 41; systems of, 13–14, 25–26; timing of data collection/reporting by, 49, *See also* Internet

Wertsch, J. V., 80

Workscapes, 15

Back Issue/Subscription Order Form

Copy or detach and send to:
Jossey-Bass Inc., Publishers, 350 Sansome Street, San Francisco, CA 94104-1342

Call or fax toll free!
Phone 888-378-2537 6AM-5PM PST; Fax 800-605-2665

Back issues: Please send me the following issues at $23 each.
(Important: please include series initials and issue number, such as EV90.)

EV _____

_____

_____

$ _____ Total for single issues

$ _____ Shipping charges (for single issues *only;* subscriptions are exempt from shipping charges): Up to $30, add $5^{50} • $30^{01}–$50, add $6^{50} $50^{01}–$75, add $7^{50} • $75^{01}–$100, add $9 • $100^{01}–$150, add $10 Over $150, call for shipping charge.

Subscriptions   Please ❑ start   ❑ renew my subscription to *New Directions for Evaluation* for the year _____ at the following rate:

     ❑ Individual $65   ❑ Institutional $118
NOTE: Subscriptions are quarterly, and are for the calendar year only. Subscriptions begin with the spring issue of the year indicated above. For shipping outside the U.S., please add $25.

$ _____ Total single issues and subscriptions (CA, IN, NJ, NY, and DC residents, add sales tax for single issues. NY and DC residents must include shipping charges when calculating sales tax. NY and Canadian residents only, add sales tax for subscriptions.)

❑ Payment enclosed (U.S. check or money order only)

❑ VISA, MC, AmEx, Discover Card #_____ Exp. date_____

Signature _____ Day phone _____

❑ Bill me (U.S. institutional orders only. Purchase order required.)

Purchase order #_____

Name _____

Address _____

_____

_____

Phone_____ E-mail _____

For more information about Jossey-Bass Publishers, visit our Web site at:
www.josseybass.com   **PRIORITY CODE = ND1**